The
M Word

MAÏA DUNPHY

GILL BOOKS

Gill Books
Hume Avenue
Park West
Dublin 12
www.gillbooks.ie

Gill Books is an imprint of M.H. Gill & Co.

Text and illustrations © Maïa Dunphy 2017

978 07171 6978 8

Designed by www.grahamthew.com
Copy-edited by Ellen Christie
Proofread by Esther Ní Dhonnacha
Printed by CPI Group (UK) Ltd, Croydon, CR0 4YY

This book is typeset in 11 on 18pt Neutraface Slab Text Light.

The paper used in this book comes from the wood pulp of
managed forests. For every tree felled, at least one tree is
planted, thereby renewing natural resources.

A CIP catalogue record for this book is available from the
British Library.

5 4 3 2 1

For Tom Laurence.
Without whom this might have been a novel.

About the Author

Maïa Dunphy is a blogger, author, broadcaster and television producer. She has written and produced for leading RTÉ comedies such as *Podge and Rodge* and *Zig and Zag*, and has made 12 female-centric documentaries for RTÉ, including *What Women Want* and *Maïa Dunphy's The Truth About* series.

She is much loved by women everywhere for her girl-next-door relatability and non-judgemental curiosity, which brilliantly explores how we live now. *The M Word* is inspired by Maïa's blog of the same name, which she set up to share her thoughts and experiences of grappling with being a new mum. Pretty soon she had gathered a large community of like-minded mums around her to laugh, cry and rant about the trials and tribulations of parenting. Covering everything from family to work and fun, *The M Word* blog now has an average reach of over 500,000 people every week.

Maïa lives between Dublin and London with her very modern blended family.

CONTENTS

PERSONAL ADS

NEW MUM SEEKS PALS

Lonely Mum seeks same for walks, coffee, wine late night chats and possibly more. Must like Bruce Willis, vodka, non-bio liquid and dreaming of the next meal. No time wasters please

Car for sale. One reck-less lady owner

HOUSE "SHARE"

Single gent seeks lady for house share. No rent. Some light house-work and "broiling". You get the idea ...

Former President Seeks Work

One time US President seeks new job. Skills include: casual racism, rabble-rousing, pussy grabbing and low IQ. Will cut hedges for food

TO PLACE YOUR AD HERE CALL 1800-FINDLOVEETC

GWYNETH PALTROW SEEKS REALITY CHECK

Hollywood A-lister seeks friend who lives in the real world for conversation, light dusting and gluten.

SEE YOUR AD HERE!

MR WONG LOOKING FOR MISS RIGHT

There's no typo. My name is actually Wong. I thought it was funny because it sounds like "Wrong". And now I've used up all my ad space. Must have own teeth

CHAPTER 17: INTRODUCTION

LET ME SET OUT my stall from the start: this is not a guide. Nor is it a self-help book, an opus of advice, a set of instructions, references or any sort of manual whatsoever. It's not even a chronological timeline of motherhood. This book is not about celebrating all of the brilliant, lovely stuff (because you'll know all about that already) but rather finding the fun in the madness and the not-always-so-brilliant.

You may have noticed that this is chapter 17. This is because when you become a parent, time, days, numbers and even reason often fly out the window. I didn't know up from down in those first few months, and so I thought, who needs logical sequential numbers? Not me. I have no use for them any more (bar admittedly when I'm trying to help my teenage stepson with his maths homework, but that kind of ruins the joke) and I suspect anyone reading this book will dip in and out of it distractedly like a Lidl catalogue (oh look, it's Greek food week!). Hence we have no need for consecutive integer chapters. Now you probably need to go and Google 'consecutive integers', which is also not the point of this book. Oh, sod it, let's agree now that we have no need for chapter numbers at all.

You may find some anecdotes within these pages at which you nod in solidarity, or that make you feel a little less weird or alone - and if that's the case, then great. Or you may end up just reading a few of the pages whilst sitting on the loo (strike that - a mother is never alone in the loo), smiling at some of the terrible drawings, and then using the book as a weight to hold a sheet over a kitchen table whilst building a den for a tiny person. And that is fine too, because I wouldn't dare to think I could impart advice or share anything even resembling wisdom on the subject of parenthood. But I do hope to start and share conversations - some important, some less so, and others inconceivably trivial (but hopefully a little funny) - that help to keep us all sane in the messy maelstrom that is motherhood.

I'm still relatively new to this motherhood lark, my son being not quite yet two years old at the time of writing. Two years in adult terms is nothing at all, I've had gift vouchers that have taken me longer to spend. That's a complete lie - I just couldn't think of anything to demonstrate how short a timeframe 24 months is. Damn, I should have gone for the best-before date on a tin of beans. Never mind ... Anyway, every stage with a first baby is a new one, and I'm still allowed to be considered a learner or to be surprised by things I had no reason to know before now.

I think we have established that I'm not trying to advise anyone how to be a good parent. There is no right or wrong way to parent. Well, actually, that's not true. There are plenty of wrong ways to parent, including, but not limited to:

- Using the passport office as a free crèche. It doesn't matter if there are 30,000 people in the queue ahead of you, a few toys in the corner and security on the door. No you won't have time to nip out and get a blow dry. Wrong way to parent.
- Letting a small child neck a pint/drive a car/juggle with knives, etc., in a bid to become a pre-school YouTube sensation. Wrong way to parent.
- Letting anyone under six choose their own food. I don't care how many celebrity parents claim their toddlers 'just adore sashimi'; most kids will just choose buttered pizza for breakfast given the choice (which is only OK some of the time). Wrong way to parent.
- Being the mother who tries to buy her seven-year-old daughter a boob job. Wrong way to parent.
- Ninety per cent of what the parents who appear on the quotidian bear-bait that is the *Jeremy Kyle Show* do. Wrong ways to parent.

So yes, for the sake of argument, there are plenty of wrong ways to parent. But my point is, the right ways are countless. There are myriad permutations and combinations of good parenting, and all are subjective, relative and dependent on so many factors. Money doesn't make you a better parent (even if it undeniably makes a lot of things easier). Having a nuclear family, a spare bedroom, a white picket fence and a swing and slide combo worthy of a theme park doesn't make you a better parent. Not getting divorced or trying to avoid being a single parent in the first place doesn't make you a better parent. Of course there are parameters, comforts, support systems and luxuries that can make parenting a hell of a lot more straightforward, but fundamentally, there will never be a one-size-fits-all approach. Once we acknowledge and accept this inalienable truth, don't berate or congratulate ourselves too much, stop judging and comparing, sneering at or envying others, then things tend to be OK. Or you simply stop giving a shit what other people think.

Modern-day motherhood is competitive. I was warned about this and in many ways it turned out to be true. But for the most part, other mothers are supportive and lovely, and often become a safety net at a time when you need one more than ever before. The online world opens

up so many new and brilliant possibilities for backup
and information, but it also leaves us prone to bullying
and undermining. We should remember that the online
community is no different to one in the real world. Walk
into a room of a hundred people and you might only
really connect with a small percentage of them – the
same applies online, with the additional complication
that the anonymous factor often drives the potential for
assholery (it's a word now, OK?) up significantly.

In all aspects and stages of life, we need to find our
tribe. We gravitate towards like-minded people from a
young age – in schools, in clubs, in first jobs and every
job thereafter, in social groups and pubs, at parties and

eventually at the other side of the school gate. But having a baby doesn't automatically mean you will have lots - or indeed, anything - in common with another mum apart from a birth story. For every person you'd like to swap numbers with, there will be a dozen you'd fake your own death to avoid ever seeing again. This is what I struggled with most when I became a mum.

I had a thriving career in broadcasting in my native Ireland, and a supportive network of family and friends, but my UK-based husband and I had been in a long-distance relationship for over six years. Long-distance can be a highly workable - and even attractive - relationship option when both parties are busy and independent, but it's not massively compatible with having a baby. And so, after much discussion and deliberation, I decided to move to London to give the full-time family option a go. For any woman, becoming a mother for the first time is overwhelming at best, but I had also left my tribe behind, and I found most of the baby and toddler groups nothing short of soul destroying. They were filled with banal chats with boring women (who most likely thought the same about me) about breastfeeding and putting names down for schools. On one occasion I scooped up my baby and walked out without saying goodbye when one woman had spent 45 minutes telling me how baby wipes had changed her life ('Honestly! Now I use them for cleaning everything from my face to the furniture!'). I went home hoping she'd somehow erase herself with them.

Yes, I eventually found some semi-like-minded mums to hang out with, but in those early foggy months, I found a virtual tribe of sorts. A WhatsApp group with my friends back in Ireland, Skype with my parents and my pal in Hong Kong, and a veritable army of women through *The M Word* blog I set up when Baby Tom was just six months old.

I had been reluctant to start a blog; I thought I had nothing original to say, nothing new to offer, and surely we had reached peak parenting blog, hadn't we? Eventually, however, I saw it as a sort of online diary, a way to keep myself sane at 4 a.m. But then something unexpected happened. People started joining in, signing up and sharing their own stories. It took a few months for me to realise that despite the fact that there were thousands of mummy-sites and blogs out there, not unlike the 'walking into a room' analogy, it wasn't just me who was looking for my tribe, but innumerable other women too (well, not innumerable, the numbers are at the top of the Facebook page). So even though I wasn't doing anything pioneering or reinventing the speculum (more's the pity), it attracted lots of women who were just like me.

It was lovely, and I found the blog so comforting in my first year of motherhood. Because it doesn't matter how old you are when you have your first baby, once that little person arrives, it's like turning up on the first day of a new job and realising you don't have the right qualifications. You feel like that chap, Guy Goma, who walked into the BBC for an IT job interview and was accidentally interviewed on the live news when he was mistaken for someone else. And so in the absence of my real friends and family, an online family of sorts sprang up.

The M Word became a website, which is now a platform for some of the other women who came along for the ride to vent their spleen, share their joy and sadness, or just take the almighty piss - all valid emotions that can materialise around motherhood. Motherhood is like getting on the best roller coaster in the world with the worst hangover of your life; but make no mistake - even if you end up with whiplash and vomiting into a bucket, you will never, ever regret joining the queue.

Jeez, that was a terrible analogy. But please refer to the opening paragraph - this is not a guide. So what is it? Well, you know those people who take ten minutes out a day to do a puzzle or a crossword? Or just play *Candy Crush* on their phone and stalk their exes on Facebook? It's a sort of book equivalent of that – a welcome distraction of mama anecdotes (mamanecdotes?) and some of the blogs from *The M Word* to distract you from the chaos, remember why you love being a mum, or just to remind you that you're not alone. It is something to dip into when you don't have the headspace for a novel (and you won't have to keep re-reading the same page because you're so tired that you've forgotten where you got to). A sort of Sudoku for the soul, if you will ... actually, that makes it sound quite intellectual. Maybe more of a word search, but a really simple one made up of nine squares with 'cat' hidden three times in it.

I think you get the idea.

WHAT IS PARENTING?
(Refrain: Buggered If I Know)

ONE OF THE MOST widely abused clichés you hear when you become a mum is some variation of 'Ah, parenthood! If only it came with a handbook!' Guess what ... it does. And it has done quite possibly forever. Some of the most rudimentary prehistoric cave drawings included tips for successful baby-led weaning (this is entirely made up but who knows).

But yes, there are thousands of handbooks – walk into any bookshop and you will see the Parenting/Child/Baby section is probably taking over a significant percentage of the building – not quite as sizeable as Cookery, but thankfully now eclipsing Celebrity Autobiography. Not unlike picking up a travel brochure or joining a cult, it's up to you to decide what direction you want to take. If you don't want to buy one of these mothering manuals, you can walk straight to fiction and buy a nice holiday read, but if it's a handbook you want, then no one can say they don't exist. The trouble with advice books of any kind is finding the right one for you. There's no point in trying to work out what's wrong with your dishwasher by reading the clock radio instructions, and equally, it's futile applying a set of rules to a baby who isn't responding to them or who needs a different approach.

What does parenting mean? A hundred years ago it meant 'keeping your children alive', and even a couple of generations ago, it just meant 'raising your kids', albeit within your own parameters, abilities and means. Sometime over the last while (I have to be vague as I have genuinely no idea when it happened) people stopped just raising kids and began 'parenting'. It became a verb with wildly varying connotations. Now we have a string of adverbs that can precede it: tiger, hothouse, snowplough, attachment, helicopter … every time I open a magazine, a new term seems to have been coined.

Nothing strikes fear into the heart of a mother like the thought of any harm befalling her baby. This isn't a new concept; we all know that fear sells like hot cakes. Hot cakes that should be kept away from babies in case they burn themselves (you see? Fear is EVERYWHERE). Google 'nineteenth-century parenting manuals' and prepare to guffaw at the hilarious and ludicrously archaic suggestions and advice. But then remember that in a hundred years' time, mothers may be chatting incredulously on their hover boards (they'll have to become a reality eventually, right?) about the things we do now:

'Those idiots let them drink from plastic cups? So toxic!'

'They let them play on mobile phones to keep them quiet! Did they not KNOW what radiation was?!'

'Can you believe they put them to sleep on their fronts/backs/sides?!' (This seems to triangulate with every generation so it's only a matter of time before we're told to suspend our babies from coat hooks to be safe.)

This gem from the book *Searchlights on Health: The Science of Eugenics* by B. G. Jefferis and J. L. Nichols published in the 1920s isn't quite what you might find in the 1980s bestseller *What to Expect When You're Expecting*:

'Pregnant mothers should avoid thinking of ugly people, or those marked by any deformity or disease; avoid injury, fright and disease of any kind.' Fair enough, lads. Sounds like something a certain Führer might have said ...

Most of the early advisors on maternity and motherhood were men. In fact, I think they all were (I can't be arsed to look it up, so if there was some legendary 'Dr Quinn: Maternity Woman', feel free to get in touch on Twitter, correct me and be subsequently ignored). The rules were simple and often similar: cuddling was bad, leaving babies to cry until their faces inverted was normal, smacking was essential, and raising children was generally not dissimilar to raising animals in a Victorian circus. Parenting was all about detachment and discipline – there were even nineteenth-century 'baby cages', a handy device for apartment dwellers that could be suspended out the window to ensure your baby was sufficiently 'aired'. Maybe that's where David Blaine got the idea.

Things moved on, and in the 1950s the idea of the 'good enough' mother was popularised by psychoanalyst Donald Winnicott, who made a connection between poor parenting and essentially every other single problem in the known world (no pressure, eh, mums?). According to Winnicott, fascism, violence, social injustice (and no doubt reality TV stars had they been a thing then) could all be directly attributed to shit parenting. So he believed that the path to a better society begins in the nursery – and he may have had a point. Most importantly, he stressed that parents didn't have to be perfect, but just had to do their best.

Then came Dr Benjamin Spock in the 1970s (that paragon of parental guidance who most of us born in the '70s were ostensibly raised by) and his more gentle approach of trusting a mother's instincts. Basically, he made millions from telling people to use their own common sense: nice work, Spock. And then followed the female experts: from Penelope Leach in the '80s and her child-centric views – you had the baby, you make the sacrifices – (tell us something we don't know, Penny), to militant maternity nurse Gina Ford and Generation X's Supernanny Jo Frost, whose 'naughty step' revolutionised attitudes to disciplining kids (and presumably, carpeting) in the early 2000s.

Recently the twenty-first century has seen parenting move into a whole new realm. There is no longer one guru, one attitude or one food pyramid. More than ever before, mothers are educated women who have built careers before having children and approach parenting as they would a job. Their attitude is 'It has to be done well'. They are parents who are better read and have access to more information than any generation before; parents who know they only have one shot at getting it right, and are determined they'll be the ones who raise the next well-balanced Internet millionaire with a sense of humour and a social conscience. Or maybe just a decent human being. Either way, as parents, we are all looking for answers when sometimes we're not sure what the questions should be.

Every century and every generation think they have parenting sussed, but we are always evolving based on new knowledge and technology. Parenthood is no different, and in our pursuit of perfection, we too will get things wrong, make mistakes and at some point our children will tell us that they didn't ask to be born (this is always a good time to take out an image of the baby cages and remind them how good they have it).

Based on all this, you might think that I have a tiny clue what I'm on about. Well, you'd be wrong, I don't. I didn't read a single book whilst pregnant (for the record, I don't recommend this approach; you don't have to read the entire library, but please read something), and only know any of this because I looked it up so I could make some cross references that weren't just my own whimsical musings.

When it comes to what sort of parent I am, I have no idea. I know occasionally I want to wrap my little boy up in a cocoon and protect him from anything even remotely negative until he's 50, and then I realise that makes me sound nuts (but it would make for a pretty amusing surprise 50th birthday party).

The truth is, I just want him to be happy, independent, funny, smart, compassionate and kind, and for that to happen, he'll have to learn some things the hard way. The most important things we can do for our kids are give them the best education within our means, teach them that being an asshole never works out well for anyone, and remind them that fussy eaters are irritating. If I can get those three things right, 'you'll be a man, my son!' (Although as a pitch for a parenting book, it may need work.)

THE RIGHT TIME TO START A FAMILY

WELL, WHEN IS IT?

This chapter should really consist of just one sentence in enormous capital letters: WHENEVER YOU START

I think it probably warrants a little more discussion, but those three words really are the only answer to the question. If you raised eyebrows by having a baby after a one-night stand at 18, or after your sixth round of IVF at 42, in time you will realise that that was the right time for you. You might quietly wish that babies had come sooner, later, or in higher or lower numbers; but rest assured that there is never a 100 per cent, cash-back guaranteed, certified 'right time'. You will never think you have enough money, time, bedrooms, headspace, career progression or hours in the day, but if and when it happens, that will be the right time.

I can't think of any other aspect of human life that incurs the unwelcome interest of other people more than fertility. Women are bombarded from all sides with statistics, opinions, facts, figures and not-so-thinly-veiled misogynistic articles in certain tabloid newpapers featuring sad-faced women warning others of the perils of leaving it too late. It makes my blood boil (although the aforementioned tabloid might say that was down to my advancing years).

Here's a newsflash: we're not stupid. We know that the optimum physical age for having a baby is probably sometime in our early 20s, but that doesn't work for all of us. Given the choice, the optimum practical age for me would have been about 75 (but then I realised I wouldn't be able to go on all those retirement cruises I'm planning, or behave disgracefully at the bingo if I had a baby in tow).

There are endless reasons why not all women have children aged 23:

- We have worked our arses off building a career. This isn't selfish. We weren't sitting in the pub for 20 years forgetting that we were getting older (well, not every day).
- We aren't ready yet. It doesn't matter what biology or imaginary clocks tell us; if we're not ready, we're not ready.
- There are fertility issues people know nothing about, and which, frankly, are none of their business.
- We haven't met the right person. Or any person. There are few things more aggravating than being asked, 'But do you not want children?' when you've either just come out of a long, wrong relationship, or are struggling to find the right one. Doing it alone isn't for everyone.

Of course this is assuming you want children at all. For many years, I wasn't sure that I did, and when I changed my mind aged 39, I was married and thankfully conceived easily (no one needs more detail than that). Up until that point, the relentless questions and comments had come at me like the quickfire round of a gameshow:

- 'Do you not want to get married?' (When I was still single at 32.)

- 'You'd better get your skates on if you want to start a family.' (When I got married at 35.)
- 'There must be a problem.' (Said behind my back when there was still no baby three years later.)

But the quizzing didn't stop there. No, sir. A pregnant woman has the unwitting ability to escalate a line of questioning from 'water cooler banter' to 'police interrogation', and EVERYONE has an opinion. It's bad enough that a lot of nice things go out the window when we're pregnant – stuff like double-shot cocktails, waterslides, mystery meat kebabs at 2 a.m. and clothes with waistbands – but what makes things even worse is the constant stream of scaremongering and unwelcome bullshit that we are subjected to from the moment there's a visible bump that can no longer be passed off as cake-bloat.

'For God's sake, woman! Are you eating a runny egg?!'

'Are those highlights in your hair?'

'You're lucky to be pregnant at your age. Was it natural?'

'Shame you'll have to put your cat down.'

'Oh, you can't use eye creams anymore, you know.'

'You haven't really put on enough weight.'

'You're a bit too fat now.'

These were just a few of the pearls of wisdom I was offered whilst pregnant by (presumably) well-meaning folk. And one of the main reasons for revealing that we were having a boy was to stop the insufferable gender predictions from strangers wielding wedding rings on bits of old string, guessing based on a Chinese chart or the size of my backside. You haven't known true degradation until someone stares at your arse and declares, 'It's a girl!

Girls ruin your figure!' And don't get me started on the daggers I received when I ordered a beer in a bar. I had one small beer at a work event – ONE – in between about 17 glasses of water, and if you judged the situation on the looks I got alone, you have sworn I'd whipped some class A drugs out of my elasticated fat-pants and injected them straight into my uterus. Do people think pregnant women do no research whatsoever? Do they think we didn't get the memo? Rest assured, we did. If it's that they feel a responsibility to unborn children everywhere, then I'd like to know if that responsibility continues when the baby arrives into the real world. It should. In fact, every person who offers a pregnant women unwanted or ridiculous advice should be forced to babysit one full day for every inane comment made. At that rate I'd have free childcare in the bag until my son is nine.

Although on second thoughts, do I really want someone looking after my child who thinks staring at a full moon will make a baby hairy? Perhaps not.

Then at last the baby arrives; maybe now we'll be left alone and the badgering will stop? Ha! IT'S ONLY JUST BEGINNING, MAMA!

- 'I heard you had a C-section? That's kind of cheating, isn't it?' (Yes. Major abdominal surgery is absolutely cheating. No other way to look at it: I'm a fraud. It's a veritable walk in the park, and I am no different to that guy who faked his own death in a canoeing accident to collect the insurance).
- 'You know I had a home water birth with no pain relief?' (Great! Your medal is in the post! Oh no, wait ... THERE ARE NO MEDALS. Just mums who want their babies in the world safely.)
- 'You're breastfeeding/not breastfeeding/combination feeding?' Translation: you need to try harder. (I am trying my best. All the time. Do you not remember how difficult those first few weeks were?)

Amidst all the madness, though, there are also lovely people, wonderful friends, overawed family, tearful dads, giant maternity pads (surprisingly reassuring, like a comfy crotch hug), smiles, sobs and so much unbridled joy when you peer into that little cot and see the little face staring up at you (even more joy if they're asleep). And these are the things you need to hold on to (except the giant pads - you'll need to let those go eventually).

Every mother has her own memories of the early weeks with her first baby, most of them now modified by nostalgia, wistfulness, rose-tinted spectacles or subsequent birth experiences. But when I visit or call a friend who is going through it for the first time, I am always mindful not to trot out the more unhelpful platitudes that did me no favours. I don't turn up unannounced, and when I do visit, I bring food that can be frozen and don't stay long. I text but don't call (but always answer if they ring); I buy smaller, practical gifts and don't send flowers (our little kitchen looked like a florist, and I wished I could have spread out the lovely bouquets over the months that followed); I ask how they are rather than asking after the baby first; and make it clear that I'll be awake at 4 a.m. if they want to chat (although this happened once and neither of us can remember any part of the conversation). I also remind them that a new baby puts an enormous strain on even the strongest marriages and relationships and to ask for help rather than expect partners to just know.

Peppered with minor disasters and small triumphs, the first couple of months with a new baby were some of the most extraordinary days of my life, despite rarely leaving the house. When I look back at the photos of me and my son Tom in those early weeks, a look of mild terror in both our eyes, I think of the things I might have done differently, and then look at him now, thriving and toddling around like a tiny drunk at a wedding, and remind myself that maybe I didn't too badly at all.

The time might not have been perfect, but it was right.

HOW YOU IMAGINED YOUR
FIRST PHOTO AS A MOTHER

YOUR ACTUAL FIRST
PHOTO AS A MOTHER

PREGNANCY

THE FEAR

I'M NOT GOING TO spend ten pages taking you through the forty weeks of my pregnancy, as there was nothing particularly remarkable about the physical side of it. All the nonsense about glowing (glowing is for those weird bioluminescent creatures that inhabit the sub-abyss of the sea - please refer to David Attenborough) and having impossibly beautiful hair (your hair doesn't actually get thicker, it just stops falling out. But then all the hair that should have fallen out during those nine months sheds at the same time after you give birth which is alarming and crap) is just that - nonsense. Nine times out of ten, the much-vaunted pregnancy glow is down to cutting out booze, quitting cigs if you smoke and eating better. Oh, and as an aside, whilst you're pregnant, even if you are well enough to go out, you will realise how toweringly boring your friends are when they're drunk.

All you need to know about the physical side of my pregnancy is that I was lucky, wasn't sick once, didn't gain much weight (despite sucking up food like a human Dyson), and for the most part, just got on with life. I didn't read any pregnancy or birth books, attend a single antenatal or breastfeeding class and kept telling people, 'Sure, I'll only freak myself out by finding out too much, and anyway, I'm too busy working'.

In reality I had my head in the sand because I was very, very anxious. I worried for pretty much the entire nine-and-a-bit months. My friend who was pregnant at the same time as me signed up to pregnancy yoga, sang to her bump, paid the price of a second-hand car on a third trimester photo shoot where she was semi-naked and her bump was draped in chiffon and soft lighting, and wore sweatshirts emblazoned with cute slogans like 'Little Peanut On the Way' and 'Pregasaurus'. I just invested in a couple of pairs of maternity jeans and bought a load of cheap tops in a bigger size and walked around slightly slouched so people would just think I was a surly beer drinker.

I worried that all of this meant that I wasn't maternal by nature – how could I bond with a baby if I hadn't bonded with the bump? What was wrong with me that I wasn't photographing myself side-on every two weeks to document the 'journey', buying a Doppler and playing Baby Mozart to my belly? None of this was a good omen for me, and if I thought about it too much, I convinced myself that something was going to go wrong. And so I dealt with it in the most ill-advised way possible: I turned a blind eye to the fact that I was even pregnant. I didn't feel I could speak to anyone about it as my husband was so excited and most of my friends were either already happy parents, didn't want kids at all or were desperately trying for babies. How could I tell any of them that I wasn't even sure I wanted to be pregnant? I realised I did want to be, but my angst about becoming a mother made me feel so lonely.

In hindsight, I wish I'd found professional help and spoken to someone about how I felt, because I think I could have saved myself a hell of a lot of worry if I'd known that how you feel during pregnancy has no bearing whatsoever on the kind of parent you'll turn out to be, and that everyone at times convinces themselves that something might go wrong. Some days my fears were crippling, I spent a lot of time alone and teary, and I'd have swapped the worry for water retention in a heartbeat. (No, you wouldn't, say those who had ankles like an elephant's).

So that's the only advice I'd like to impart on pregnancy. All the medical stuff - the morning sickness, exhaustion, constipation, heartburn, birth plans, etc. - will be covered by your doctor at various appointments along the way, or discussed *ad nauseam* by well-meaning friends. And sure, aren't I the smug cow who didn't have any of those ghastly side effects, so what would I know about them anyway?

You won't find this book laden with chat on trying for babies, trimesters, timelines, kicks, nausea, cravings, scans or all the other weird, wonderful and leaky things that happen during pregnancy, because they are all so relative and subjective. There is just the message that if any of you did or do feel like I felt, then rest assured you are normal, and that not painting your bump to look like a Kinder Egg doesn't mean you'll turn out to be a terrible mother. Because guess what? When my son arrived, my love for him increased incrementally hour by hour and day by day, and it still continues to, to the extent that I wonder if my heart will need to have doubled in size by the time he's 18. (Although I am regularly reminded that the teenage years may plateau the love index a little.)

Anxiety is a monster, and can eat you from the inside out. Don't ever be afraid to put your hand up and ask for help.

THE
ADVICE

—

HAVING PROMISED that I won't be dragging anyone through a monotonous reminder of the Forty Weeks, there are a few less-important aspects of pregnancy that are worth an honorary mention: advice, for one. I never expected to get so much of it – the majority unsolicited and unwanted. It started about three minutes after I told people I was pregnant and continued relentlessly, like a nine-month tornado of bilge. (I was once even sent a photo of someone's damaged vagina in the name of advice.) I listened to most of it politely, smiled and nodded begrudgingly (except for the photo, which arrived by email from a colleague I had worked with ten years ago. There was no nodding and smiling when that rosy gem popped up in my inbox).

Advice (however well-intentioned) before you have a baby is a form of nostalgia from the person doling it out, and nostalgia isn't what you need at a time like that. Large bags of crisps, yes. Other people's wistful memories and partial regrets, no. The ones I bristled at most were the lists of all the things I should be doing 'whilst you still can'. These included (but were not limited to) eating out, lying in, going to the cinema, reading books, more sleeping, leisurely strolls and weekend city breaks. Having a picnic featured surprisingly heavily.

Really?

I think picnics are a pain in the arse – surely they were invented to entertain kids once you have them; that, and to prove a couple are in love in Merchant Ivory movies. I am deeply suspicious of any couple in real life that goes on picnics. If I wanted to get sand in my teeth, drink lukewarm wine and eat cold sausages, I'd hire a wind machine and do it in the comfort of my own home.

Around the seven-month mark, I'm embarrassed to admit that the whole 'do it while you still can' itch started to scratch, and I began to panic at all the lists of things I should be doing which were by now burning a hole in my brain, and said to my husband, 'We have to go to the cinema IMMEDIATELY! And then walk home the long way, stop for a romantic meal and then have a lie in tomorrow. WE MUST HAVE A LIE IN AND THEN GO TO PARIS!'

Not for the first time, he looked at me like he had just seen the last of my marbles rolling away in the distance.

And then it struck me.

I was 39 years old.

I had been on a lot of walks, travelled around the world, eaten lots of popcorn in the cinema, been on many city breaks, danced til dawn many times (well, about five times, truth be told) and rarely surfaced before 10 a.m. on the weekends (people do understand that sleeping hours can't be stockpiled, don't they?). I'd had 20 years of the fun stuff, and although I hadn't forgotten how great these things were, I was ready for something new.

Now that I am on the other side of pregnancy, I don't tell pregnant pals who've come after me to do things they have probably done plenty of. They know sleep will be limited for a while and that spontaneous meals out and tequila shots at 2 a.m. might be non-starters. But here's the thing: you don't actually miss these things as much as others think you do, and they don't stop altogether, they just take a bit of planning.

Once I found my stride with my baby, I was happy to take him with me to most places. I discovered a new list of things I wanted to do. We found baby-friendly film screenings, went for walks, hung out in the park and got to know each other. It was lovely and at no point was I pining for a city break (just to be clear, I wouldn't turn one down now, though). Fast forward a couple of years and I have a child-free lunch out with a group of girlfriends every couple of months, and a few times a year, we call in all favours and plan a girls' night away. Yes, life changes and things are different, and like all exhausted parents, there is almost nothing I wouldn't do for more sleep, but at no point do I look back and wish I'd spent more time having fucking picnics.

THE CLOTHES

'MATERNITY STYLE': can we all just accept that it's one of life's inalienable oxymorons? You may have had (as I did) a naive sartorial plan in those first few months when you didn't have a clue what was ahead, inspired by photos of a perfectly pregnant Blake Lively and her ilk in glamorous dresses that accentuated their bumps. Until I learned the cold hard truth about normal-shaped pregnant women and fashion. It's oil and water, people, oil and water.

For the most part, the first few months are relatively simple as you can pretty much stay in your own clothes (bar THOSE jeans). Also, you may be so overwhelmed or violently ill that you don't give a shit anyway. Then in the second trimester, you simply ditch any fitted clothes you may have still been shoehorning yourself into, invest in a pair of those joyous elasticated-waist maternity pants, buy a few big tops and embrace kimonos. If you work in an office, they'll have to just suck it up. If you don't work outside the home, hell, your family are lucky you don't just cut a hole in a duvet and wear it like a poncho all day.

But all this is academic until you have to attend an event or occasion where you actually want to look nice. It could be Christmas, a birthday or a wedding. Something that will be committed to photographs and, worse, social media for years to come.

Don't stare, Peter.

But it's the guy from Big Momma's House!

In my last few weeks of pregnancy I went to a wedding and was determined not to look like the star of *Big Momma's House*, so took my ever-widening torso to a specialist maternity clothes shop where the prices nearly sent me into an early labour. (I know there's a bit of extra fabric, but I was still only dressing one person.) No, sir, I was not spending €300 on a dress I would never wear again. So I lowered my expectations and scoured the high street instead.

The first thing I noticed was that the majority of maternity gear looks like it has been made out of all the fabric left over from the 1980s. I suspect there's a fabric mountain somewhere, piled high with floral and paisley prints that no designers wanted post 1991, which is now sold off on the cheap for maternity wear to make pregnant women feel not only more pregnant, but more shit in general. Unlike non-pregnant people, we don't have many options, so have to accept the ugly fashion crumbs we are thrown.

I persisted and tried on dress after dress, each one more hideously unflattering than the last. Just trying them on felt like trying to throw a tarpaulin over a patio table in the wind. In the end, I cut a hole in my best duvet cover and wore it like a cartoon Mexican bandit. No, not really. I bought a black maxi dress online for about €20, a few sizes bigger than normal, and told anyone who would listen that I was massively pregnant and hence couldn't wear anything else. I think they were all relieved when I went home at 11 p.m.

I don't know what the lesson is here, or if there even is one. Maternity clothes are thankfully short-lived and pregnant women are simply not a priority for designers, which you can understand since it's difficult to dress people shaped like Mr Greedy. And for the pregnant, fashion just isn't as important as we thought it might be in those last few months so we accept it and move on.

When your baby arrives, you are so enamoured by all the impossibly cute little outfits, your own fashion fails fade into insignificance. Until it's six months later and you realise you're still in those elasticated pants. But they can stay.

THE MATERNITY WARD

NATURALLY, before you meet your baby, you have to get it out of your body. As promised, I won't bore you with the ways and means. Maybe you'll have a water birth at home with no pain relief and bake a cake afterwards, maybe you'll need an emergency C-section or maybe you'll have your baby in the car on the way to hospital. But more than likely, you'll end up in a maternity ward at some stage and, all the usual hospital rules aside, I wish someone had warned me about the inevitable clash of personalities that would happen there.

Midwives and nurses are extraordinary people who should be paid the same as boom-time property magnates (although if that were the case, they'd probably all be living off-shore at the moment, which would be no good to us). Yes, midwives and nurses are wonderful people. Have I made that über-clear? Great, now I can add, 'having said that', which, as we all know, usually leads to an about turn. Every mum I know has a story of the midwife whose cup of tea or kind words at just the right time were a godsend, versus the one who made them feel as if they had wronged them in a previous life.

Maternity wards are unusual places, and the staff and patients populating them are different to those you'd find in any other hospital ward. For the most part, patients are hopefully not sick and are there for life-changingly exciting reasons. (On a tangent, I was told that you don't have to check your dignity at the door when you have a baby, but you kinda do. In the heel of the hunt, it doesn't really matter and it's nothing they haven't seen a thousand times before.)

Most mums-to-be are bright, opinionated and perceptive; women who know their own minds. When it comes to birth, they know what they want, or equally, what they don't. But many lose their confidence the second they

walk into the maternity ward. I know a lot of mums
have stories of empowerment and taking control during
childbirth, and I swear if I have a second baby, I will try to
be like them, but when I walked in through those swinging
hospital doors, I forgot EVERYTHING. From what I can
remember, all I did was thank everyone profusely all the
time and look terrified. Even when a midwife brought in
a team of trainees to stare at my naked lower half and
discuss lochia (trust me if you need that one explained,
you don't want to know), I just nodded and smiled like
someone newly arrived in a country without being able
to speak a word of the language.

I didn't know any of the midwives or other staff in the hospital I was in; they were strangers on whose kindness I relied. And most of the them were very kind indeed and I deferred to their knowledge and experience. But the first 24 hours with a newborn is like nothing else on earth. You run a gauntlet of emotions and feelings, wrapped up in that strange post-birth euphoria and pain. And every couple of hours or so, a midwife or nurse pops in and checks on you, and they are like angels. Angels bearing smiles and hopefully toast.

But at least once in your hospital stay, you may meet the midwife at whom you'd like to throw the unfeasibly large maternity pad in your hospital bag. In my case, it was the one who kept telling me I was letting my baby 'run rings' around me already. I was only in the hospital for a total of 48 hours, but my stay unfortunately managed to coincide with two of her shifts. She referred to me as an 'old first-time mum' (tell me something I don't know, lady), and twice told me to pull myself together when I was weepy and struggling to feed my son. These may not sound like big things, but when you're exhausted, in pain and concerned that you're already messing things up, they feel monumental. And then she lost my respect forever by telling me I couldn't have any toast.

Unfortunately still, the same midwife was on duty when I wanted to discharge myself from hospital. She handed me a couple of toilet seat covers (which are like inverted cardboard top hats) into which I had to 'prove I had gone to the loo' before I could leave. I managed to go in the cardboard bedpan of indignity, but when I was finished, she had gone on a break.

I can't describe how keen I was to leave, so I picked up my top hat of shame and headed off down the corridor to find her (or anyone else qualified to sign me out in exchange for a glimpse of my cardboard toilet), the contents sloshing dangerously from side to side.

Eventually I found her, and she peered into the bowl before reeling back in mild disgust. 'You only had to do a wee in the hat, Ms Dunphy,' came her sharp reply.

I made the long walk back to my room as quickly as I could while carrying a cardboard hat full of shite. I did make it home that day, and like all the other less-pleasant sides of birth, this episode was quickly resigned to history and funny pub anecdotes.

Although it's important to be respectful and courteous to all the staff in a hospital, it's equally important that it works the other way, and so if someone's tone feels wrong or upsets you, speak up. (And maybe consider packing a toaster in that hospital bag.)

THE EARLY
DAYS

THE FOG

SHORTLY AFTER HAVING TOM, my first (and still only) baby in 2015, I was quoted in an interview comparing the sleep deprivation that comes with having a new baby to that of being detained in Guantanamo Bay. My heart sank when it was published. It had been an attempt at humour; a throwaway comment never intended for public consumption. The complaints would surely come fast and furious; after all, how could anyone compare the magic of motherhood with the brutality of a controversial detention camp, even in jest? I was crestfallen, as I didn't have the energy to deal with the inevitable troll-filled fallout ... but then a strange thing happened - no one complained. No one retweeted it in disbelief or told me to cop on, not even so much as an angry emoji face from an anonymous Twitter egg. Now, of course, there's every chance that no one cared, but I think it's more likely that a nation of mums smiled and nodded to themselves with their exhausted eyes half-closed, thinking how an orange jumpsuit might actually have its practicalities.

I've heard the first few months with a new baby referred to as the 'fog', the '100 days of darkness', the 'post-natal abyss' or the 'black hole' ... all more reminiscent of a sci-fi B movie than a description of what is supposedly the most meaningful time in a woman's life. I say 'meaningful' rather than a list of superlatives because, although most new mothers will have crossover tales from those early days, not all of them find it exhilarating or wonderful. At least not all of the time.

You can't prepare for those early days and weeks with a new baby - especially your first. Yes, you will be sore, exhausted, tearful, confused (and that's just before midday) and wonder if you will ever feel normal again. There will be days you feel on top of the world, and others when even a well-meaning stranger peering into your pram makes you want to run for the hills. You will want to punch people who tell you to 'enjoy it because it goes so quickly', but then, mark my words, it will go so quickly and you will wish you enjoyed it more.

I think one of the reasons women have more than one baby is so they can do it again and relish the magical newborn phase unfettered by the fear that came with the first (although it's just not the same with an older child hanging out of you too). But don't look back and berate yourself for not having loved every second or reacting like a superwoman at all times. Ask for help, accept it when it's offered and be kind to yourself. The cocoon in which you find yourself encased will soon dissipate, and you will have to deal with the real world again, so for the love of God, accept a few casseroles for the freezer.

VISITORS

—

THE FIRST THING you need to brace yourself for with a new baby are the visitors. With a first child, the onslaught of visitors can feel like one of those fight scenes from *Lord of the Rings* where a charging army of uninvited orcs appears over a hill (but bearing gifts of rattles and soft pram blankets). Just remember that if you have subsequent children, the same visitors will probably do no more than send a text, so maybe it's best to suck it up. Partners need to step up at this point, and be mindful of when and how many visitors are enough for you. If they don't automatically assume this role, ask them. There is one exception to this rule, though, and that is with in-laws: six letters, two little hyphenated words, but always one massive reaction. The staple of many an un-PC comedian's routine for pretty much all of the twentieth century, and whilst we've come a long way since Les Dawson asked us to 'take my mother-in-law …

please', there is nothing like the arrival of a new baby to expose the cracks in even the strongest of family unions.

I was fortunate to have my own mother move in with us for the first six weeks, which was a godsend. She was there every day, good natured and non-judgmental, cooking and minding all of us. My own in-laws are wonderful people, and visited after a couple of weeks, stayed a couple of nights, cooed over the baby and left again, not feeling pushed out or rejected.

A good friend wasn't so lucky. She had her first baby a few months after me and, like mine, her mother came to stay for the first few weeks to help out. She said that despite her husband doing his best, if it hadn't been for her mother, she doubts anyone apart from the baby would have eaten in those first insane weeks. But then her mother left and her husband announced that now his mother would be coming to stay. She tried to explain that this is not how the post-baby visitation system works – mothers stay, mother-in-laws just visit – but he was adamant. He saw it as a quid pro quo situation and said it was only fair that his mother stayed the same amount of time. Now, I'm sure many people have wonderful mothers-in-law, but my pal knew she didn't have one of those.

On arrival, her starter for ten was this gem: 'Oh, but Stuart* is looking so tired. I hope you're not expecting too much of him?' (*Name changed beyond all possible recognition.) Actually, Stuart did look a little peaky as he had been out at a boozy work dinner the night before, whereas my friend's only time off baby duty in over a month was at a doctor's appointment to be re-stitched. You haven't known true exhaustion until you consider having your vagina repaired like a torn jacket pocket to be a break.

What ensued was three weeks of every judgmental mother-in-law cliché in the book. She wasn't holding the baby correctly, wasn't putting her in enough layers, was making a rod for her own back with the lack of routine, etc. What made it doubly irritating was that the criticisms often weren't direct, but instead conveyed via talking loudly to the baby:

'Well now, I see your mummy must want you to have nappy rash as she hasn't used nearly enough Sudocrem.'

'No wonder your daddy is looking thin when your mummy is so busy with you.'

'Oh, doesn't your mummy have it so much easier than I did in my day!'

For the full 21 days of her stay, my friend sucked it up. But once mammy-in-law had left, she thought on reflection that it had almost been worth it, just for the feeling of relief once it was over. Everything else seemed manageable now.

I shared this story with a group of women and opinions were divided. One woman had lost her own mum before her first child arrived, and said she would have been lost without her mother-in-law. Another said she always reminded herself that one person's mother is another's mother-in-law. A third pointed out that as we all now had children, hopefully we would be mothers-in-law one day. This was the part that jarred the most – we were all mothers, so it stood to reason that we might indeed one day be mothers-in-law. We hesitated, looked at each other, laughed, and then ordered another bottle of wine.

We'll cross that bridge when we come to it.

THE
BORROWERS

'NEITHER A BORROWER nor a lender be.' I'm sure most of us have heard that saying at least once in our lives (usually from the kind of family member who starts the sing-song at a wedding, or trots out phrases like 'What's for ya won't pass ya by!'). It was Shakespeare who coined the phrase, advising that to borrow or lend something to a friend can often result in losing both the thing loaned and the friend.

But borrowing and lending makes the modern world go round, and usually we know the rules. If someone asks for the loan of a tenner, we know it needs to be paid back. If a friend asks if she can borrow that dress you wore last Christmas, we know it should be returned promptly (and dry cleaned). And we all understand how borrowing from the bank works (unfortunately).

It struck me after Baby Tom arrived that an awful lot of borrowing and lending goes on around babies (which is understandable when you find out the amount of crap you have to buy), and then the rules become far less clear. If you borrow a car seat, are you borrowing it for the whole length of time that you will need it, or just until you can afford one? How long is too long to hold on to it? Is it a loan or a gift? Did that pal stop sending you Christmas cards because you never returned her changing table? Is it like squatters' rights - after a certain number of years, can you claim ownership? It's a risky business.

As I was based in London when Tom was born but still travelled to Dublin regularly for work, I had to double up on many purchases, which made life very expensive. And then there was my parents' house to kit out too as they took him a lot whilst I worked, and that would have meant tripling up on the basics, or lugging enough stuff around to rival a travelling circus.

One of my oldest friends, Caroline, (oldest in years that I have known her, not age) lent my mum a rake of baby paraphernalia, which I greatly appreciated. A cot, a walker and various other bits and pieces. As I understood it, I would return the items as and when we were finished with them (unless requested sooner). But another friend of mine who found herself unexpectedly pregnant again was seething when she found out that the cot she had lent a neighbour had since been passed on to someone else, and there were too many degrees of separation (and baby stains) to ask for it back. Another had borrowed a twin buggy offered by a friend, but was berated for the wear and tear on it when it was given back two years later. She was guilted into replacing it, which meant she may as well have bought herself a new one at the start.

Kitting out your baby is an expensive business, and often friends and neighbours will have attics and garages full of stuff that might lessen the burden. But what are the unwritten rules of borrowing and lending baby gear? Or is it like in the movie *Fight Club* where the rules are: there are no rules (yes, I know that quote is apocryphal)? Here's my understanding of this unexpected mothering minefield:

- Never accept anything offered after a few drinks. They may not mean it and will ask you weekly if you're 'finished with it yet'.
- If an item is offered to you, don't assume it never has to be returned. Even if years have passed, offer it back to the lender, and for the love of God, don't give it to someone else without checking first. This is the equivalent of getting involved in a parenting Ponzi scheme.
- Even if a friend says she won't need something back, an unexpected pregnancy automatically calls in all loans. If this happens, offer the item back immediately (even if you still need it).
- Don't be offended if you offer a new parent something and they look horrified and tell you they're 'buying all new things for the baby'. Wait until they start seeing

the price tags mount up and they'll come cap in hand: 'About that security gate ...'

- I shouldn't have to say this, but if you are returning something, CLEAN IT! You haven't known true horror until someone returns a high chair covered in food and possibly shit stains.

Ah yes, Shakespeare never warned us about shit stains.

PLACENTA
AT THE PLAY
CENTRE

AT ONE OF MY FIRST post-baby check-ups (held in a clinic based in my local play centre, which I always found disconcerting as I'd rather not have known what noise stages lay ahead), I met two women in the waiting room who were discussing their boosted energy levels. Keen to know what pearls of wisdom I may have missed out on thanks to my lack of preparation, I joined in the conversation - only to find they were extolling the virtues of consuming their own placentas.

This remains a contentious topic for some, but for those of you who might be faint of heart, fear not; they didn't serve it up with fava beans and a nice Chianti, but rather signed up to the fairly recent trend of placenta encapsulation (where the organ that kept your little one going for 40 weeks is desiccated and put into capsules to take as a supplement). Many believe consuming our own placenta boosts energy, lifts moods, can help avoid depression and increases milk supply. I say 'believe' because like so many things thrown at new mums, it's so very dangerous to make claims and promises around such a vulnerable time in a woman's life.

I'd always thought that once the baby is delivered, the placenta's job is done. That's why your body gets rid of it; it's nothing more than a pile of slightly grisly meat – the kind of weird cut chefs could do something fancy with, but the rest of us would just throw into a slow cooker with a tin of tomatoes and hope for the best.

Advocates of placenta consumption tell us that animals eat their placentas post-birth hence so should we. But for animals, this is simply a matter of survival; they need to remove all traces and smells of a new baby to avoid detection from predators. I don't think this applies to us – at least, I hope it doesn't. And frankly, the 'well, animals do it' argument doesn't really wash; there are plenty of things animals do that we don't, either because we have evolved not to need to, or because we now have indoor toilets (although stag nights are often exempt from these truths).

The two women asked me what I did with my placenta, and I suddenly felt oddly embarrassed to admit that I didn't even see it after birth, which was my decision (I say 'decision', but in those moments, they could have removed my feet and I would barely have noticed). I have no idea what happened to it, and I can only presume it was incinerated (or judging by the grim beef casserole I had in the hospital canteen the following day, maybe it wasn't ...).

But here's the thing: if it makes any woman feel better to keep her placenta in the freezer, eat it like a steak or have it freeze dried into a supplement, once all the health and safety rules are applied, then THAT IS OK. (Just please don't do what a woman in the US once did and sneak it into a lasagne for a dinner party, not telling diners what the mystery ingredient was until after they'd eaten.)

The problem I have with it comes back to the same old boiler plate of false claims being made to women at what can often be their lowest ebb. One of the women from that waiting room had been told categorically that she could have avoided the crippling postnatal depression she experienced with her first baby had she only consumed her placenta. She became obsessed with the idea that she only had herself to blame for not having had the foresight to know this in advance, which is a big bag of very unhelpful bullshit.

So if you went home with your jar of placenta pills and felt all the better for it, good on you. But equally, don't berate yourself if, like me, you relied on a bar of chocolate and a chat with a good pal for the same outcome.

WHAT DO YOU DO ALL DAY?

—

I PREVIOUSLY BELIEVED this string of six little words to be a myth propagated by magazine articles; surely no one ever actually spoke them out loud? Even in the 38 years before I had a baby, it wouldn't have occurred to me to say them to a new mum, or any mum for that matter. Even when I was young and naive and used to drink shots at 4 a.m. and wished I could stay in bed and not have to get up for work. Even then.

But when Tom was eight weeks old I bumped into a guy I used to work with who, as a result, knew how insane my work schedule used to be at times. We said hello, got the obligatory pleasantries about the weather and how cute my baby was out of the way, and then he hit me with it.

'So what do you do all day?' (I realise that's seven words, but the 'so' was an unnecessary interjection so I discounted it).

It took me a good ten seconds to process the question. Someone had actually said it. To my face. A real person who wasn't a complete asshole asked me what I did all day with a hint of envy in his voice. Because after all, I was on maternity leave, which is basically a six-month 'staycation' filled with afternoon naps, coffee, daytime telly, cake and playing with your new favourite person in the world.

I resisted the urge to punch him.

But, for some reason, I began manically trying to list off what I did all day. 'Well, I get up at 6 a.m., usually after no more than two consecutive hours' sleep in between feeds, and at least one change of clothes for me and the baby. Then I have to get the baby fed, unload the dishwasher, wash and sterilise all the bottles from the previous evening and overnight, then strip and wash his sheets, then get him back down for a nap, after which if

I'm lucky I might find ten minutes for a shower, but then he wakes up too soon so I don't. He needs another bottle then so I get him dressed but he has reflux so we both end up covered in sicked-up milk at least four times a day and have to change ...'

After I'd reached about 4 p.m. on an average day without pausing for breath, I realised how insane I sounded and the whole exchange was becoming very awkward.

'Sounds terrible,' he said.

'Oh no, it's lovely,' I replied defensively, despite knowing I had made it sound like modern-day slavery.

He made his excuses and left sharpish. The moral is this: never ask a stay-at-home mother what she does all day. Just don't. Just be envious of all the coffee and cake and naps if that's what you want to believe. And if you're a mum who is asked this question, go for the punching option. You can blame it on hormones in court.

MAMA MILESTONES

AS A NEW PARENT, many people only ask you about your children. Sometimes it's because you have nothing else in common and there's only so much to be said about the weather and politics, but usually – admittedly – it's because they are genuinely interested. But in the early days of new motherhood, I was driven to distraction by the constant quizzing on whether or not my son had hit various 'milestones'. It started early on with well-meaning neighbours and supermarket randomers alike:

'Is he holding his head up?'

'Has he started smiling yet?'

'Any sign of a tooth?'

'Is he crawling?'

'Not walking yet, I see?'

'Is he on solids?'

'Is he a good eater?'

'Is he smoking yet?' (Just checking that you've stuck with this ...)

'Is he out of the Moses basket/your bed/into his own room, etc. yet?'

'Still no teeth then?'

'Has he said "Mama" yet?'

The list is endless, as any new parent will pay testament to. But they often only serve to either A) state the obvious (one lady in a check-out queue asked me if my baby had a tooth yet whilst he stared up smiling with what was clearly a mouthful of gums), or B) make a new mum worry that her baby isn't doing things at the right time. Woo hoo! More stuff to worry about!

However, it is far more important that we measure these junctures in parental points rather than baby ones. I call them Mama Milestones, and reaching each of them is so significant. Think about it - your baby will reach each landmark or breakthrough in his or her own time. There's not much you can do about that - no amount of playing peekaboo will make a tooth appear quicker or see that first step taken. But Mama Milestones are not only inextricably linked to those of the baby, but possibly even more significant for everyone's welfare. So instead of asking mums about their babies' development, I ask about their own:

'Have you managed to leave the house on your own yet?'

'Have you stopped needing a cushion to sit on at all times?'

'Have you mastered breastfeeding in public without taking off virtually all your clothes?'

'Are you out of the giant maternity pads yet? You'll miss them when they're gone.'

'Have you perfected leaving the house without forgetting at least two important things?'

'Are you back wearing bras that don't unhook like festival hammocks?'

'Has the absolute fear that you're doing something wrong lifted yet?'

'Have you handed over money to pay for something in a shop, realised you have baby poo stuck under two of your fingernails, and not been sick with horror?'

'Have you got on a bus with the buggy?'

'You went to a café, fed your baby, met a pal for coffee and got home without crying and had a lovely time?'

'YOU'VE GOT THIS!'

I look back on those early days, and as much as I remember every single one of my baby's milestones, I'm also pretty proud of my own. I remember the day his reflux stopped and I could finally go out wearing half-decent clothes. The feeling when I took on two buses and a train to meet my sister for lunch and being almost confident about it. Getting through our first flight alone at only eight weeks. When he cried his eyes out in a restaurant and it didn't make me panic and want to pay for everyone's lunch. The first time I went alone to a mum and baby film screening, him in a car seat, and me with my coke and popcorn, feeling genuinely relaxed.

Baby milestones will come in their own good time. But sometimes it's us who need reminding of how well we've done when we hit our own.

BLUE IS FOR BOYS...

SOME PEOPLE have strong opinions on the traditional 'blue is for boys, pink is for girls' conventions, and others don't give a monkey's. The truth is, many parents dress their new arrivals in conventional colours, simply because the clothes are cute. Listen, I'm not claiming to have a masters in Gender Studies, but I dressed my baby boy in blue simply because I liked the clothes.

Yet I lost count of the number of times he was mistaken for a girl. I had his insanely thick hair cut into a 'boys' cut' (whatever that is) from when he was ten months old, and I shamelessly adhered to dressing him in blue. Small blue trousers, blue t-shirts, blue jackets, blue PJs with dinosaurs and tiny trucks on them with just the occasional pop of red and green for the hell of it ... you get the idea. This was all very 'traditional', so I was told, but it still didn't stop people thinking he was a girl. It didn't bother me in the SLIGHTEST when someone did; I get it – babies all look like babies. Tom wasn't asking for a Scotch on the Rocks in a deep voice in a gentlemen's club somewhere, and so it's understandable that someone might be unsure of his gender despite his mother's archaic attitude to dressing him.

But what's funny about gender mix-ups is not that they happened, or even my reaction to them (which I think was always pretty casual), but the reaction of the person who made the mistake. Nine times out of ten, instead of chuckling too and saying 'ohsorryboutthat', they tried to defend their blunder. I remember one incident on a train that went a little like this:

Random lady on train: Oh, what an adorable baby! What's her name?

Me: Tom.

RLOT: Tom? Is she not a girl?

Me: No, 'she's' a boy called Tom.

RLOT: Then why did you just say she?

Me: Sorry. I was just trying to be funny. He's called Tom. A boy called Tom.

RLOT: You just never know these days.

Me: You never do.

RLOT: Even though you've dressed him in blue. Lots of people dress girls in blue.

Me: They might. But he's a boy dressed in blue.

RLOT: I mean, he really, really looks like a girl.

Me: OK, but trust me, he's a boy.

RLOT: I do trust you. Why would you lie?

Me: I wouldn't. I'm just making a point.

RLOT: Have I offended you?

Me: Not in the slightest.

RLOT: Because he really could be a girl. It's not my fault.

And so it continued until she got off the train.

Another woman I met on a plane made the same mistake but then berated ME for 'being so old-fashioned' by dressing him in blue.

'You never know who he might want to be,' she told me.

Um, what?! He can be whoever he wants to be, lady, but I don't think me dressing him at six months old in a blue all-in-one with a picture of a tractor on it is going to force him to deny his sexuality in years to come.

There is a lot of gender neutrality out there and that's fine. There are little boys with cascading curls and girls with crew cuts, boys in pink dungarees and girls who love trucks. And that's ALL OK! But whereas initially there was a mild backlash against such gender neutral attitudes, often now the ire is being directed towards parents who choose to stick to a 'traditional palette', for want of a better description. And don't get me started on parents whose children genuinely choose 'gender-specific' toys.

Gender is not a black and white thing – we finally know that, and are learning more every day. For some people it's fluid and changeable, or not what other people might think. But when he was tiny, in my son's case, it was just a blue onesie with a tractor on it.

ALL MOTHERS ARE IDIOTS

FOR WORK AND PERSONAL REASONS, I am a frequent flyer, and have been for nearly a decade. It used to be a breeze, but since having a baby there is no doubt it's slightly less simple and certainly more costly (but I would say I make at least the price of one flight in ten back on the amount of Tom Ford perfume I use from the airport shopping tester bottles). I think people – with or without children – will understand that travelling with kids is no mean feat; hell, even going to the supermarket often turns into an epic worthy of its own military campaign-inspired title. Operation Dessert Storm or something (note to self: idea for book title).

But despite the fact that mothers have to become twice as adept, skillful and diplomatic when doing anything with children in tow, others don't always see it that way, and some folk see a buggy and automatically assign the pusher a lower IQ or common sense levels.

It was at the automated check-in machines in an airport one week that I realised it. I have used these machines countless times – sometimes they work, sometimes they are temperamental and you have to queue up at the customer service desk. That is fine, but tends to subtract from valuable airside time that you may not have left enough time for.

Many times, pre-baby, these machines didn't work for some reason or other. And if I asked a staff member for assistance, they would presume I knew what I was doing and assume that the fault was with the machine and not me. But same scenario with baby in tow, and I suddenly noticed that instead of waving me off to customer service, the well-meaning chap would talk to me as if English wasn't my first language: 'HAVE YOU PUT THE RIGHT NUMBER IN? AH, WOULD YOU LOOK AT THE LITTLE FELLA? DO YOU HAVE THE RIGHT NUMBER? DID SOMEONE BOOK FOR YOU? ARE YOU OFF TO VISIT FAMILY?'

And then, all at once, it hit me; this wasn't new. It had happened a lot since a baby became my accessory du jour, and suddenly, like a crap deleted scene from a Jason Bourne movie, all the incidences came flooding back at once: at the train ticket machine, in the bank, at self-check-out counters, and at many other places where my basic abilities had previously never been called into question (bar DIY shops where it was always assumed I didn't know a Rawlplug from a ratchet).

I wondered, was it just me? I will acknowledge that as a very new mum, there were times when I must have looked terrified in public with a newborn (those first few tentative trips out with a first baby are nothing short of terrifying), and maybe that could have been misconstrued as not knowing how a sodding ATM works (ironically, those were the times when no one offered me any assistance at all). But as someone whose basic life skills were never questioned before, I wondered, was it the buggy or something in my face that implied I didn't know what I was doing? Did I look like an unfortunate child raised by wolves whose life suddenly depended on having to navigate an automated ticketing system?

I regularly bemoan the fact that not enough people offer mums a helping hand. But a hand with the engineering of parenthood is not the same as the assumption that we somehow can't cope with (or never knew in the first place) the logistics of everyday life. Quite the opposite: since having a baby I now know that if mothers ran the world, it would be a much better and significantly more organised place.

WHAT'S YOUR ROUTINE?

IN THOSE EARLY DAYS (or months, realistically) of motherhood, there was one parenting question I dreaded above all others, and unfortunately it remained one of the most frequently asked by friends and strangers alike. No, it's wasn't 'Jesus, you look wrecked. Are you not sleeping AT ALL?' It was the ubiquitous 'So what's your routine like?'

It seemed to be a conversation filler, the parental chit-chat equivalent of discussing the weather with taxi drivers, but also a question I never knew the correct answer to. That's the reason I hated it. I didn't want to show myself up for the mum-spoofer that I was: the novice, the making-it-up-as-I-go-along chancer. Answering the question ran the serious risk of exposing all of my parenting shortcomings.

The thing about a baby's routine is that just when you have your head around it, it's time to start a different one – you don't just stick with the same routine for 18 years (more's the pity). The first weeks with a new baby are nothing but chaos, but then one day you realise you have it: sterilise, feed, wind, wash, repeat. You've got a routine and it's working! But then it's time to drop one element and add another. I often only discovered what the new component was when someone looked surprised by my answer to the routine question and replied with things like:

'Oh, you haven't dropped the night feed yet?'

Shite. I didn't know I was supposed to.

'You're still doing two naps a day at this stage?!'

Bugger. Not from tomorrow I won't.

'You haven't moved to cow's milk already?'

I will as soon as I get home.

'You should really have introduced flash cards by now.'

You are not someone I ever want to see again.

The answer I always really wanted to give to 'What's your routine?' was 'We get up. I try to keep everyone alive and then we all go back to bed again. Somewhere in between those three things I try to find time for the million other things I have to do.'

Does that count as a routine?

So, have you got a routine?

Oh yes!
Get up.
Try to stay alive.
Go to bed.

Having more than one child inevitably means a routine kicks in. I know that the weeks my school-going stepson is with us, the day has a natural start, middle and end. It's formulaic, the way a working day used to be. But when it was just me and The Baby, 'routines', like rules, were made to be broken.

Everything got done. Eventually. But sometimes naps were missed, hair wasn't washed, baby was brought into parents' bed at 4 a.m., dinners were a bit later than they should have been (or were half take-away), bath time was overlooked in favour of cuddles on the couch, or bad traffic meant baby started the night sleeping in a car seat.

Sod it. I did my best. I started each day with an ideal scenario and ended most of them with an acceptable amount of compromise. Routines are for choreographers.

WELCOME TO YOUR NEW LIFE

YOU 2.0

CONGRATULATIONS! You've made it through the early days and things are starting to feel normal again; well, a new kind of normal. A very, very new kind of normal.

Although motherhood changes you permanently, I have always believed that it doesn't fundamentally redefine you. My default setting has never been calm. It's something I've tried to work on for most of my life, but to a certain extent, I have to accept that being a worrier is part of who I am. Which is why I thought motherhood and the new life that would come with it might not be for me. I had worried about all the possible negative outcomes without fully comprehending the positives. I had seen parenthood turn previously calm, together, competent, smart women into be-tracksuited calamities. I'd watched them unable to return to work or go anywhere without at least six weeks' notice. Of course, I realise now that, being a catastrophist, I was cherry picking the bad stuff without seeing (or being able to see) the good side.

When I was pregnant, I was in a panic about work. I didn't want to give it up. I worked in an erratic industry where I knew flexi-hours and part-time just wouldn't be an option. I confided in a friend about how afraid I was and that I was trying to put other work in place that I could do from home. 'Forget about it,' she said. 'Trust me, you won't care nearly so much about work when that little man arrives. Motherhood completely redefines you, there's nothing you can do about it.'

This was the worst thing to say to someone like me. I was 39. I had only known the normal me for a long time and I didn't want to be redefined. I didn't want to be told there was nothing I could do about it.

Giving advice to women pregnant with their first baby is a tricky business. They need reassurance, not warnings; support, not condescension – however well it is intended. They need to be told that everything will be fine, but on their own terms. Concern is relative – one person's worry is another's irrelevance.

Of course two years on, and work has indeed taken a back seat. And not just a regular back seat in a car, but several rows back. The back row of the bus back seat. And I'm more than happy to keep it there for a while. My friend was right in some ways, but wrong in others. Motherhood hasn't redefined me (except in the acquisition of the title 'Mum'); I still have the same sense of humour, like the same food, and work is still important to me, although admittedly, not as important as it once was. I prefer to think of it as a rebranding. A sort of Me 2.0. An upgrade if you will. I'm still a worrier, but the perspective that comes with a baby means I no longer entertain trivial concerns (but they have been replaced by plenty of others!).

I would never tell a worried mum-to-be simply not to worry because soon she'll be redefined. I don't dismiss the concerns she might have about work/her relationship/her body/birth, etc., and give that wry, smug smile that says, 'Soon you'll find out what the rest of us know!' Because now I know that although mothers have so much in common, we are all still as individual as we were pre-parenthood. All I needed to hear when I was pregnant was that everything was going to be OK.

Although admittedly, there is one thing motherhood just might have redefined permanently: my waist.

POST-BABY BODIES (Yawn)

—

IN THE GRAND SCHEME OF THINGS, we know the 'post-baby body' rhetoric is very unimportant, but even so, how we feel about ourselves is important, and how we view ourselves shapes that.

Here's a newsflash: women's bodies change after the oh-so-simple act of growing an entire new human (or multiples thereof). We know that, the advertising industry knows that, the media knows that, etc. etc. ... it gets so dull. I honestly believe that women are more accepting of their post-baby tums than the world would have us believe. I certainly am – I'm amazed at what my body did, and I'm way too tired to worry about cellulite anymore.

However, I have noticed amongst my mum pals that there comes a time when you have to accept that certain changes you thought might be temporary are, in fact, not. Most of us have a wardrobe full of clothes that we hope we will be able to get back into eventually after having a baby (for economic reasons as much as anything else), but every woman usually undergoes at least one physical change that she must eventually accept.

For one of my friends, it was that her feet went up a size. She assumed they would revert to their usual size five, but alas, four years after having her last baby she has finally accepted that she needs to bin her old shoes.

Post-Baby Bodies

For another friend, it was accepting that even though she weighs the same as she did pre-babies, she is now a different shape. She used to be an hour-glass and now she's 'more of a pint glass' (her words).

Another friend still was left with a post C-section 'shelf' (an area of overhang above the scar), which no amount of magical creams or exercise has shifted. She can no longer comfortably wear tight jeans (but has a newfound love of gorgeous dresses).

My moment of fact-facing came a year into motherhood when I looked at all the pretty bras in my drawers that I can no longer fill, and finally accepted that I may, just may, have gone down a size permanently (not a great thing when you were hardly in mountainous territory to begin with) and went to M&S to get re-measured. '34A', came the reply. I'd be happy for that to be my bus route, but now have to accept that the Bs are gone for good. It's actually something of a relief as wearing my old bras was like trying to transport quails' eggs in a regular egg box, so at least now everything fits and I can just get on with it. I did feel a little cheated, though, as I had been told there would be a particularly glorious moment of pregnancy when for a golden month or two I would be as curvy as Kelly Brook (well, from the waist to collar bone at least), before I just looked obviously pregnant. I know it sounds a little vain, but I looked forward to it – one of the few perks of pregnancy.

But those halcyon days never came. Yes, they got marginally bigger, but not significantly. I never had that brief window of finally filling a bikini. That self-esteem-boosting month many friends had told me about, before your belly obscures your view of the ground but when your boobs look like something airbrushed in a lads' mag, was never to be mine.

My husband reassured me that I was in proportion. And when I growled back at him, he tried to console me by reminding me that if my boobs never inflated then they'd be unlikely to collapse after the fact. I took heart from this. I had been warned of the post-pregnancy, post-breast-feeding crash that for many women resulted in boobs like a spaniel's ears/wet hiking socks/canvas 'bags for life' left out in the rain/(insert your own description here). But me and my mini-jugs would avoid this fate – and I took solace in that.

Except it happened anyway, and now my boobs look like birthday balloons left hanging on a gate long after the party is over.

I'm not really complaining though, because of course it was a fair trade ... and you can do extraordinary things with padding these days.

No, sir, these little permanent changes really aren't important. They are not part of the constant onslaught of 'post-baby body perfection', and not about putting yourself under pressure. Be it stretch marks, giant feet, tummy shelves, a dress size or shape you weren't before, or deflated boobs; accepting the new you and moving on gives you just one less thing to worry about. And do yourself a favour and get rid of clothes that don't do you any favours anymore, because it's just another stage in life, like when you grew out of your school uniform. And if you still have that in your wardrobe, we need to talk.

LONELINESS & THE 'MUM FRIENDS'

BEING A MUM can be incredibly lonely. It was something I had heard mentioned in vaguely hushed tones, but as someone who has always spent a lot of time alone - both working and living - I never thought it would affect me. Also, I thought having a baby would be the opposite of lonely. I wouldn't be physically 'alone' for years to come; heck, I can barely go to the loo alone these days, but guess what? It is.

Tiredness in itself is an isolator. When you are so exhausted that you can barely dress yourself, you'd often rather not go anywhere at all, even if you have the option. If you worked before having kids, the lack of daily adult conversation and company can be jarring (you may even miss the dull chats you previously tried to avoid with creepy Barry from HR at the water cooler). You could find the connection you had with your partner isn't quite the same, or you might resent them for going back to work when you can't, or sleeping soundly whilst you breastfeed for the fourth time during the night or get up for the sick toddler. You might have lots of great friends but they're all busy at different times, and our jobs/families/lives aren't always in synch. Blink and a month can go by and you never did meet up for that coffee. You may find that some days your only interaction with people is the half an hour you grab to scroll through your Facebook feed – oh, you have hundreds of friends there, but a hashtag doesn't replace a hug.

In my case, it was made doubly hard by moving to a new country at the same time as having a baby, compounded with a husband who was away a lot. There was one week in particular when I didn't speak to anyone for nearly four days. On the fourth day, I met our elderly neighbour on the doorstep, and when she said good morning, the reply that fell out of my mouth made no sense whatsoever. It was only then that I realised I hadn't spoken out loud –

bar baby speak and singing A-B-C slightly out of tune - for some time. I closed the door and burst into tears.

But I knew I wasn't alone. I saw other mums pushing prams and buggies - some with their heads down, striding purposefully, others trying to make eye contact. I never noticed them before, but suddenly I did and so always gave them a smile. Occasionally they looked at me as if I were a cartoon lunatic, but sometimes we'd stop and chat. Two strangers knowing that a five-minute exchange might just make all the difference to us both.

I had heard the term 'mum friends' many times before having a baby. Some of my best pals from school or college who became mothers long before me would reference them in a sort of dismissive tone as if I wouldn't understand. 'Who's Julie?' I'd ask, thinking there was no one my best friend knew who I didn't. 'Oh, just a new mum friend', my pal would reply, and I would raise an eyebrow suspiciously as if I'd caught her cheating. Of course as the years went on, a sort of divide naturally appeared between those who had kids and those who didn't. It was only to be expected; I still had more disposable income, wanted to go out on Saturdays and lie in on Sundays, whereas my friends with babies ... well, now I know exactly what they spent their weekends doing. It doesn't mean I lost any friends, but I just watched them move in a different direction and gravitate towards new people going through the same thing, and I had enough people left around me to still do mine.

But it was only some months after becoming a mother that I really saw the importance of mum friends. I had lots of them back in Ireland, but because I had moved to London just before having my baby, I had to start from scratch. And I realised that trying to make mum friends was a lot like dating; and I always hated dating. The do-they-fancy-me looks across bars followed by the

will-they-call-me mornings spent staring at phones that
didn't ring. I had to go through it all again albeit it in
a slightly different way. Mums are just people too, after
all, and like how when you walk into a bar there's no
guarantee every person there will fancy you, just because
you and someone else both gave birth doesn't necessarily
mean you'll like each other.

A few well-meaning pals set me up on mum-friend blind
dates. 'Oh you'll love Gina, she's had a baby too!' But I
didn't love Gina. Her voice alone made me want to shove
my head under water for a very long time. We had nothing
in common at all, and by the time our coffee and cake was
finished and we'd shared our birth stories, I knew I didn't
want to see her again and I suspect she felt the same. We
went Dutch on the bill with no arguments so there wasn't
even the pretence of 'Oh, I'll get the next one.'

Then there was Sandra, who lived close by and decided
that I was going to be her friend whether I liked it or not.
I actually hid behind the curtains one day, almost afraid
to breathe when she knocked on my door. We will never
be friends.

At the early baby groups I signed up to, I initially found
no like-minded mums at all. At one, I downed a cup of

tea so fast to get away that I scalded my throat. Still, not being able to swallow for three days was a fair exchange for escaping the clutches of the Most Boring Woman in the World (*Guinness Book of Records* pending).

Then there was Debbie. Beautiful, funny Debbie, who I still think about wistfully. We met briefly in the waiting room for baby health checks. All the times I'd been there previously, not once had I had a laugh with someone in the waiting room. But then she was there, and she said, 'You'll never know if that was me or him,' when her baby farted, and no one else laughed but me. I guffawed. I only found out her name as she was called in before me, but when I came out of my appointment, she seemed to be waiting for me. OK, she was feeding her baby, but still, she could have left and done that elsewhere. She HAD to be waiting for me, right?! And so I hovered around her like a teenage boy at a disco and made small talk and we laughed some more. I wanted to ask for her number, but I didn't know how this mum-friend dating scene worked. So I eventually tapped my watchless wrist and said I'd better make a move. Was there a flash of 'please don't go' in her eyes? I paused for one more beat and then turned to go. She called out a goodbye and I wondered one more time if I should ask her if she wanted to see me again.

Ah, the naive, early days of mum-friending. Now if if I meet someone lovely, I ask if they'd fancy a coffee sometime. If they say yes and give me their number, I can be sure they like the cut of my jib too. If they pause and say, 'Um, you can find me on Twitter', it's the mum equivalent of giving someone the wrong number in a bar.

Here's my number. Give me yours and we can do everything together!

Umm... I'll Facebook you.

Having pals in the same boat as you can be a lifeline. Of course, there's no need to say goodbye to your old friends (it's another essential lifeline altogether to ensure you still have non-baby time and conversations if you can) but there's no denying that things change dramatically when you become a parent, and relationships across the spectrum reflect that.

But the Mum Friend Experience has another variant beyond deciding who to forge friendships with and who to avoid, and this is the 'how to ditch someone who won't take no for an answer' situation. Most people can take a hint – I'm sure I have more than once been the person someone else can't be bothered with – and if my attempts at contact are ignored, I let it go (I hope). But there is a breed of person out there who will not take 'no' for an answer, like a tenacious terminator. I've been warned it gets worse when kids start school, and occasionally who your child forms a friendship with can end up like Russian Roulette for the parents. You may well meet pals for life or just fun acquaintances through your offspring, but you might also end up barely slowing the car down when you drop off their child after a playdate for fear of being asked in. Again.

Hey! Couldn't see you there for a second! Wait...are you hiding from someone?

Umm...no, I've just taken up car mechanics.

The worst possible outcome here is when your initial, sleep-deprived bad judgement lets you down. Maybe you met a fellow mum, thought she was great and swapped numbers. Fast forward six months and you realise not only do you have nothing in common, but she is actually the biggest irritant since that pure wool sweater you refuse to throw out. But this isn't like ghosting someone on social media, or taking yourself off Tinder. This woman knows you're a stay-at-home mother and worse still, KNOWS WHERE THAT HOME IS AND IS DETERMINED YOU WILL BE FRIENDS. She can't take the hint and the biggest calamity is your children are now friends. So what do you do? Move house? Take your kids out of school? Fake your own death??

We have to remind ourselves that this time is so precious and very short. Mum friends are important, both existing ones and new ones – for every ten mums you meet, one might be a potential pal. But even the other nine might just be what you need to get you through a lonely day. Or at least fodder for all your fake friends on Facebook the next day.

MOTHER & BABY GROUPS

I DO THINK mother and baby groups deserve a section all of their own. They can be a vital resource for a lonely mum (especially one like me who had moved country), or for someone whose other friends are working or at different stages in their lives. Either way, initially, the very thought of them went through me. Yes, I knew it would be good for me and the baby to get out of the house, but I had never been one for clubs or groups growing up, and at nearly 40, it felt a bit late to start.

Many women tell me that they met their new BFFs at one of these classes, and even my own mum reminded me frequently that she met many of her friends for life through us when we were little. So I bit the bullet and signed up for a baby swimming class. With the benefit of hindsight, I should have started with something a little more simple, a coffee morning or 'meet other mums on a walk to the letterbox' group. Basically anything that didn't involve swimming in winter. But I'd paid up in advance and the first class loomed large so there was no going back.

I read the introductory notes start to finish several times. People who work in childcare often speak v.er.y s.l.o.w.l.y a.n.d c.l.e.a.r.l.y and it turns out leaflets aimed at new parents are somehow written the same way, so there's no possibility of crossed wires or misinformation, both of which are vital when dealing with tiny incontinent people and a communal swimming pool. I bought the special swim nappies as instructed. In fact, I bought two sizes just to be on the safe side. I bought the neoprene safety pants that go over the nappy (it's a belt and braces situation, folks - see previous comment about incontinence and pools). I packed two towels for my baby, two changes of clothes in case something dropped on a wet changing room floor, and a small travel hairdryer so he wouldn't have to go out in the cold air with wet hair.

The morning of the class arrived and I packed snacks and warm milk in a thermos; nothing had been left to chance, this was a bag of glory. And then it struck me: I had forgotten swimwear for me. In my attempts to pack the Perfect Baby Swim Bag, I had completely neglected to include anything for myself. I have never been a swimmer or a beach person so I didn't keep a stash of bikinis to hand, and the only thing I had was a never-worn maternity tankini. I usually eschew clothes with the word 'tank' in them, but as the only alternative was swimming in my underwear (which we've all done at some stage in our 20s with varying degrees of humiliation), I had no option but to pack it. It would be fine, I told myself; sure, it was just a bit of splashing in the shallow end, wasn't it? All it had to do was stay up.

It turns out Baby Swimming involved more bouncing and spinning than I'd anticipated, and the maternity tank-travesty was about as practical as cutting two holes in a plastic bag and stepping into it. I watched in horror as my massive pants floated away like an angry jellyfish on the second bounce, unable to grab them what with trying to hold the baby above water and everything. The worst part was that no one else spotted my mishap so I had to keep bouncing around in the circle of shame praying that I'd catch up with my embarrassing jetsam before anyone else. I didn't. Someone else's baby got caught up in them like a tiny innocent dolphin in a shark net. I think all the other mums were most appalled by the fact that I had appeared not to have noticed that I was naked from the waist down. Their reactions told me we wouldn't become besties who'd laugh about this over mojitos some day.

I transferred to a different swimming group the following week. And bought a new swimsuit.

Unsurprisingly, I didn't sign up for a second term of the overpriced, underwhelming swimming classes (but not before being fleeced for the underwater photoshoot). But like Grizzly Adams, moving on at the end of each episode, I kept searching for new baby groups in the hope that one would be revelatory, or if nothing else, at least my baby would learn to socialise with other little ones, and so I persevered. (I've just remembered that Grizzly Adams had to move on at the end of each episode as he'd been wrongly accused of murder, so maybe that wasn't the best comparison.)

The next one I tried was a local weekly playgroup, and on our arrival the organiser greeted me as if she was certain English wasn't my first language:

'NOW MUM, WE ASK THE ADULTS TO TAKE THEIR SHOES OFF HERE.'

Yep, I can see that.

'MUM MUST KEEP AN EYE ON HER LITTLE ONE AT ALL TIMES, OK?'

Gotcha. I wasn't planning on nipping to the pub.

'WE HAVE TEA-MAKING FACILITIES, MUM, BUT YOU MUST NOT BRING HOT DRINKS OUT OF THE KITCHEN BECAUSE YOU MIGHT BURN THE LITTLE ONES.'

It was the last one that got me. I understood it was a health and safety issue, but they must have realised that every mum in that room made hot drinks at home on a daily basis. Sometimes ten times before 10 a.m. I also understood that perhaps - not dissimilar to having to pay attention to how the seat belt works on an airline safety demo regardless of how often you fly - it was a legal requirement and our friend was just doing her job. Even then, there were ways of conveying the rules to the parents without TALKING AS IF NANA DIDN'T HAVE HER HEARING AID TURNED UP.

A few weeks later I gave another group a go. This time it was run by the local church, and the second I walked in I could see that it wasn't nearly as well organised, equipped or financed as the previous one. The toys had seen better days, those that required batteries were without, and it certainly wasn't staffed by anyone who looked like they had a qualification in childcare. But then it happened: one of the older women who ran the group wheeled in a trolley bearing hot flasks of tea and coffee and tins of biscuits, and in a normal, NON-SHOUTY voice, said with a smile, 'Help yourselves, and I'm sure you're all well used to looking after your children so I needn't give you the safety drill on hot drinks!'

With that she had me. I accept that it didn't take much to piss off a frazzled mum, and maybe I was too harsh on our slow-speaking safety consultant at the previous group, but no matter. Life is about finding your tribe, even in the everyday, and for a couple of hours on that cold Monday morning, that lady with the trolley and the common sense was in mine.

I eventually came to the realisation that finding your tribe may be the point of these classes for smallies who have yet to form the ability for cognitive memory – they are more for the mums (and occasional dads). I didn't believe that my ten-week term of floating Tom on his back singing 'splash splash splash!' would make him a shoo-in for the 2032 Olympics any more than I thought attending a Mini Mozart Masterclass (yes, I was sent a flyer for that gem. I think the tagline was 'Make a maestro of your mini-me!') would give my son musical abilities he might otherwise never realise.

Maybe most parents know this already, but I didn't. When I decided not to sign up for that second term of swimming (also because it was winter and involved me getting two buses in the cold), one mum told me I could be setting my son up for a fear of water. Another said I may have already left it too late to maximise on his mathematical potential by not attending the Babies & Numbers group. Another friend and I brought our babies to an interactive morning promising 'music and colourful themes' – I don't even know how to describe it – a kind of cut-price, fancy-dress son et lumière for the under-threes, if you will. We both agreed that even our babies seemed to pull unimpressed faces at the over-enthusiastic instructor. Truthfully, the most fun we had was going for tea and chats afterwards.

I called bullshit. Not on all of it, and I'm sure many mums have stories of how their babies thrived in the Buddhism for Under 2s classes. I persevered with a few and eventually found a play café that ticked all of the boxes; it gave me the chance to hang out with a few like-minded mums and share some cynical eyebrow raising over a cuppa, and my little man (toddling by this stage) had a bit of freedom, played with people his own age and had his first essential taste of minor bullying.

So give them a go, or if you're on maternity leave, remind yourself that you may not get the chance in the future. But see them for what they are: the chance of a bit of adult company and a break from the monotony; but equally, know that it's more for your sanity than your baby's future success. And if your entire week is divided up into classes for someone who wears shoes the size of mice, then you may need to have a word with yourself.

OUTBREAK

I HAVE SEEN many of my friends who are parents regularly floored or left housebound and pale by various grim-sounding conditions brought home by their children - like that angry little stowaway monkey in that film everyone forgets they've seen, *Outbreak*. 'Virus', they'd tell me on the phone as I was warned to stay away for the tenth time in as many months - that catch-all term to describe any non-life-threatening malady a baby/toddler/child picks up at a faster rate than Donald Trump picks up parody Twitter accounts.

My best pal has a constitution tougher than a Christopher Walken movie character. I rarely remember her being sick in the 25-plus years that I've know her. We travelled a lot together, ate in many a dubious street market in South East Asia, worked with exotic wildlife (I got a weird tropical disease, she didn't), accepted drinks from strangers (do not try this at home, kids) and ate out-of-date food when cash was tight. On top of that she then became a zookeeper, for the love of God. Surely you'd think working with animals day in day out would yield at least one attack of E.coli or roundworm. But no, she was strong as an ox – until she had her babies, then suddenly she picked up colds and tummy bugs the way we used to pick up deals at the off-licence.

But still I thought my son and I would escape unscathed. He was uniquely hardy, was never sick and I imagined him as a child version of that Bruce Willis character from whatever film it was in which he couldn't be hurt. (Not *The Sixth Sense*, I know he was dead in that.) *Unbreakable.* My son was unbreakable. When I told my friends this (in a more prosaic way – I'm not a complete lunatic), they all – ALL – laughed and said, 'But he stays at home with you! Just wait until he starts playgroups or nursery!'

They all had tales of viral infections with weird names that sounded like they belonged on an airport poster warning of the dangers of not declaring you'd been on a farm: 'slapped cheek', 'hand, foot and mouth', 'pinkeye' … Jesus, who names these ailments? I'm presuming they all have fancy Latin names too, but it's as if Dr Seuss came up with a more does-what-it-says-on-the-tin nomenclature for kiddy viruses to make it simple for exhausted parents:

'What does he have?'

'Oh, you know, the one that makes their hand swell. "Massive hand", I think it's called.'

But I shook my head (internally if that's possible). Not my little Bruce Willis. They would see.

Fast forward several months and, although he still hadn't set foot (or mouth) in a crèche or nursery, we had begun to go to play cafés and baby groups; places where toys trundled towards you covered in the snot of a hundred toddlers. Where your little one happily trotted around waving something in their hand with delight before eating it. What the hell was it? A rice cake that had presumably either been in the mouth of another child minutes prior, or possibly walked in on the sole of someone's shoe. Where by the end of the session, everyone left looking like they'd just survived a mucus and cornflake bomb attack.

It's not rocket science – even the hardiest mum is never the most rested person, and no amount of antibacterial hand wipes will save you all of the time. The more tired you are, the lower your defences, and a sleep-deprived parent usually has an immune system to match the bags under their eyes.

And so ended my naive smugness. Although we have so far avoided all the weird Dr Seuss illnesses, we've both had dodgy tummies a-plenty, vomiting, regular

Oh my GOD! What happened?
Have you been attacked??

No, no, I'm fine! I've just been to
a Crawlers & Explorers play group.
Off to make dinner now...

squits and random high temperatures. I have been the
grey-faced zombie mum in the pharmacy more times
than I can remember, describing symptoms only to be
told knowingly, 'Viral. Lots of fluids and Calpol' (whilst
throwing in some Imodium for myself).

When he does start nursery, I'm buying both of us
biohazard suits. Or maybe that homeschooling idea I was
throwing around might be a runner.

WEANING

I HATE the word 'weaning', it sounds too much like 'whining' or 'weevil', and is one of the many words you will probably never, ever use unless you have children (other words include: perineum, engorgement, colostrum – it's a lengthy directory). In the initial few months and years with a first baby, you will reach every milestone in your own time. Sometimes it can feel that just as you have found your rhythm, it's time to change it again, like starting a new job you have to train for from scratch every few months. Of course, if you have subsequent children, you'll feel like a pro, but even then, you will find that each one of them is completely individual and may need a different approach.

I was determined to be a laid-back mum, but I remain convinced that it is virtually impossible to be as laid back as you'd planned with a first baby. I found myself panicking about what passed my baby's lips the second he started chewing on his own foot. We are bombarded with subliminal (and not so subtle) messages about what we should feed our little ones. Organic, fresh not frozen, not too much dairy, lots of dairy, no eggs, for-gods-sake-don't-give-him-peanut-butter; and I confess to feeling nothing but dread when the time came for solids. I could cook, I ate healthily (most of the time), I understood basic nutrition; so why was I so terrified? Because it was yet another milestone to fail or be judged on.

Baby Tom had no interest in solids at six months so I waited a while. Then I introduced baby rice (he swore at me with his eyes), puréed root vegetables (not too bad until he tasted parsnip and his head almost inverted with disgust), and because I travelled so much, some commercial sachets of baby food ('What? You fed your baby that muck?!').

The first couple of months of solids were almost like going back to the start of the newborn stage. I didn't know what he liked, and I was afraid to be out for too long in case he wouldn't eat the food I had packed. And then there was an epiphany (well, that's a bit dramatic but work with me here). I had spent three hours preparing different combinations of puréed organic veg for the freezer and as a result, had barely any time left to cook for myself and so I threw together an old store-cupboard staple of noodles and whatever was left over in the fridge. As I sat down wearily to eat, Tom perked up. Out of interest, I offered him a small bit of my dinner and if he had had teeth he would have bitten my finger off.

And that was it. He became a 'great eater' and began eating whatever I did (bar the almost daily Magnum Double ice creams) and my days of standing bewildered in the supermarket were over. My life was easier, my baby happier and I stopped spending the price of a pint on an organic butternut squash. I soon found myself bursting with pride when people remarked on it, as they watched him wolfing down a plate of food that they wouldn't have a hope in hell of getting past their child's lips.

All mums want what's best for their children, that's a given. But there is so much competition and scaremongering around diet and nutrition that it has become just another thing for us to feel shit about. My friend's first baby was eating mackerel pâté and olives at eight months old. We were in awe of whatever gastro-magic she was working, but fast forward four years and her second baby will only eat bread, pasta and cheese. She didn't do anything differently, but what we seem to forget is that babies and children are individuals. If they hate the taste of mushrooms, they hate the taste of mushrooms. No amount of making a symmetrical dinner-face out of them will change that.

I once met a chef who ran a Michelin-starred restaurant and when anyone said, 'Oh, your kids must have amazing palates!', she always pretended she'd left the grill on so she could remove herself from the conversation. She had the exact same battles as any other mother, and told me she often fell back on tinned spaghetti on toast. What did people expect her kids to eat? Truffle-infused veal with a sippy cup of jus on the side? That's as illogical as someone expecting the child of a dentist to grow teeth quicker (well, not quite, but I like the comparison).

Then there are the mums who wear their babies' diets like badges of honour. I met a woman at a rare party I went to, who said she had overhauled her diet by including 'ancient grains', and so was doing the same for her two children, 'Lots of quinoa, buckwheat and chia; like the Aztecs,' she boasted. (It wasn't well received when I pointed out the average life expectancy of an Aztec was about 40.)

I never want to judge any mum (apart from the aforementioned 'like the Aztecs' one, she was a pain in the arse), because I genuinely believe we are all just doing our best. If you have the time to cook simple meals from scratch, and give your babies the chance to try new foods, great. If your children love their pizza bases made from cauliflower, kudos to you. If your kids will eat nothing but mashed potato, then don't stress too much, it won't last forever. If you're often knackered and reach for the pasta and cheese grater, give yourself a break.

No one likes a smug parent. We all know a smug parent and we all think we are not one, but sometimes the lines between pride (which is acceptable) and smugness (not acceptable; see above) become so blurred that one can veer unwittingly into the other. It's not our fault - parenting is exhausting and all-consuming and we have to take the

good stuff when we can. If your baby is the first to walk/
talk/do basic calculus, you are naturally entitled to be
proud. The danger is, talk about it too much with other
parents whose babies are still crawling/babbling/using
Granny's abacus to bash in a teddy bear's head, and the
pride can begin to smell distinctly smug.

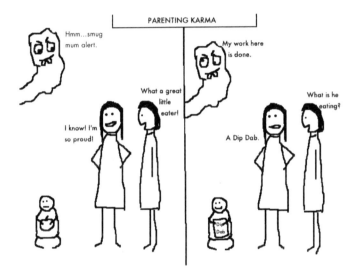

And that is exactly what happened with me, Baby Tom and
the weaning. The little sod lulled me into a false sense of
security and led me down a one-way street where the only
possible exit was smugness. A few months into our food
adventures, he was amazing: avocado, grilled vegetables,
fish, sweet potato ... He loved all the things self-loathing

adults who've destroyed themselves over Christmas eat in January. He was practically a 'clean eater', for God's sake! I already had the cookbook planned in my head: *Paleobaby and Other Wins* (working title).

My pride soon came before a fall. It slowly turned to smugness as I watched other mothers' faces drop as they told me of their kids who would only eat powdered gravy. But I was forgetting one important truth: parenting karma will always keep you in check. No sooner had I given some poor woman the head tilt as I saw her baby throw a wobbler over a yoghurt than Tom morphed into a baby who would have probably been accepted onto *Freaky Eaters* (the TV show that once featured a guy who would only eat cheese cut into tiny circles using a Hula Hoop potato snack). Almost overnight, Tom's eating transformed. Avocado could piss right off, vegetables were given as warm a welcome as an abandoned ticking suitcase at an airport, my homemade risottos were tipped onto the floor, and I began succumbing to feeding him cheese on toast rather than spending another hour crying over a piece of grilled pepper.

I kept telling myself it was a phase. Either that or he was playing mind games with me, as his new food dislikes were directly proportional to the number of tiny pots of food I had lovingly prepared and individually frozen for him.

Hello! What's that your baby's eating?

Quinoa and chia tartines. Yours?

Um...circles of durum wheat on a
bed of grilled pain de campagne.

It's spaghetti hoops on toast, isn't it?

Yes. Yes it is.

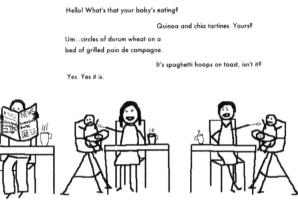

I remember sitting, crestfallen, in a café opposite another mum, watching her feed her daughter some sort of quinoa salad whilst Tom opened his miniature sandwich, took out the tomato and flung it on the floor. She gave me a genuinely friendly smile and said, 'Fussy eater?' Smug cow, I thought. Just you wait.

Things improved and as with every other aspect of parenting, we had good weeks and bad ones – some days he would eat everything put in front of him, and other days only a big bowl of pasta would do (hell, I guess he's just human that way). But food is fuel, and we obsess over it too much. I used my common sense, tried to avoid giving him too much salt or fat, encouraged healthy eating, introduced new foods as and when I could, and everything slowly fell into place. I no longer berated myself if we both ended up eating pizza whilst sitting on the floor, and didn't congratulate myself too much when he ate half a banana.

So by all means make chia seed puddings if you want to, but equally, don't forget that the term 'superfood' was invented by a marketing company.

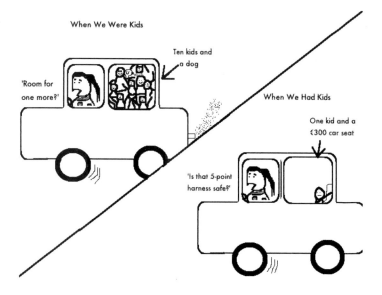

GETTING ON WITH IT

NO EXCUSES

—

SOON YOU FIND YOURSELF reaching the point when people stop treating you as a new mother, and it's time to just get on with it. I reached this point when Tom was about 18 months old, and people began to correct me and say, 'Ah sure, he's not a baby anymore, he's a toddler!', which I took to mean I should probably have my shit together by now. But, whatever, it's all semantics - he'll still be my baby when he's 25 (I just won't refer to him publicly that way).

But if I am really honest, there's another reason I liked telling people that I had a baby. We all know we shouldn't judge anyone (as if we would ...), but having a baby means you're off-limits. It allows you to get away with more, gives you license to look dishevelled, leave crap events early (or turn them down altogether), and go to the shops with hair like a bird's nest (truth be told, I always did this, but never had a valid excuse), still wear maternity jeans, eat cereal at 5 p.m., and legitimately ask a friend to make you four lasagnes when they ask if they can do anything for you. (Apropos of nothing, the word 'lasagne' gets weirder the more you look at it).

Of course, you can do all of these things at any stage of life or parenthood (and frankly I don't know how anyone with multiple kids with different schedules isn't just driving around in a dressing gown all day with a pile of sandwiches and Pro-Plus in the boot), but when you have a baby, you're off the hook from any level of expectation whatsoever.

I hated padding around the house in my slippers the week after my baby was born. I felt confined and discombobulated. I wanted to get out for a walk or just do something that felt normal. I was, of course, adjusting to a new normal, but now I think back to those days fondly and wish I'd enjoyed them more.

When you tell someone that you have a baby, the natural response is 'Oh lovely! How old?' The answer you give to this question will then yield a number of possible reactions. If you are, for example, in the supermarket looking like you may have been sleeping rough and you reply, 'Two weeks', the person asking will be dazzled by your brilliance. It doesn't matter what you look like, here you are out and about and coping with life when you gave birth to a tiny person fourteen days ago. Hell, that person has food in their fridge older than that. You are winning at life. However, if you look up through bleary eyes and say, 'Six', the reaction will be decidedly unimpressed. Six? As in years? Jeez, shouldn't you have this by now? Or at the very least, not be wearing stained clothes?

Yes, if you want to get the best reaction, just keep the numbers low. This is why I decided to keep telling people I had a baby until he starts school, if for no other reason than to justify the bags under my eyes.

The other option is to up your own age. I once told a taxi driver that I was 49; he couldn't stop telling me how amazing I looked for my age and I didn't have to mention a baby at all.

HA! The joke was on you, buddy.

I think.

MUM
CLOTHES

AT SOME POINT in the first few years of your baby's life, you realise that you now often choose comfort over anything else. But as I was a fairly low-maintenance dresser beforehand and never worked in a formal environment where I had to wear clothes that required anything more than shaking after washing, I didn't expect things to change all that much. I had always only had two hair styles: left down or in a pony tail. I could only wear really high heels if someone was going to lift me from a car to a bar stool, and looked like a dog trying to walk in socks if I had to get to the toilet at any point in the evening (you get the idea).

It seemed I was wrong. When Tom was about 18 months old, I bumped into an old colleague who I hadn't seen since he was born. Now admittedly, I was running to the shops on a non-work day, so was dressed down (i.e. one up from nightwear), but the second thing she said after 'hello' was 'Ah, who's dressing like a mum now!'

Sorry, WHAT?

I was caught off-guard. I glanced down to check myself, I was wearing jeans (which I had had for years) and a sweatshirt (ditto). OK, so I was modelling a trainers-and-sock combo that was erring on the side of Forrest Gump, but still. The clothes I was wearing pre-dated my baby, so WHAT GAVE ME AWAY?!

For the sake of full disclosure, I'll admit to a small stain on the sweatshirt (a massive stain), the jeans were starting to go baggy at the knees (from all the kneeling and picking up of stuff and small people), but still. Was 'dressing like a mum' even the insult I had taken it to be? Maybe I just looked more relaxed, more grown up, more comfortable in my own skin. (Who was I kidding, this was not meant as a compliment.)

But then I did a very odd thing. Instead of finishing the brief conversation and heading off on my merry way, I said (a little too loudly), 'But I'm wearing really amazing underwear.'

My erstwhile colleague looked nonplussed. The elderly lady in front of us in the queue, however, looked horrified. And the man working at the till raised an eyebrow.

In reality, I was wearing mismatching, slightly faded underwear that I had grabbed in a hurry, and I HAVE NO IDEA WHY I EVEN SAID THAT.

She was stumped, smiled at me and mumbled 'that'snicewellI'dbetterbeoffseeyounowmindhowyougo', and couldn't get away fast enough.

There are times when I can think on my feet, blurt out a comeback worthy of a stand-up shooting down a heckler, but unfortunately this was not one of those times. As I walked home (slowly, so as not to pass the horrified elderly lady who was walking the same way), I wondered why I had been so bothered about the comment. What did dressing like a mum mean and why was it a bad thing? Did the horrendous style-vacuum that is maternity wear create a divide between the old me and the mum-me, and no matter what I wore after the fact, I was doomed to forever dress 'like a mum' in some people's eyes? If she had seen me without my baby in tow, would she have said that? It's not as if I ever dressed like Liz Hurley at an Elton John party to go to the shops.

How I Planned to Dress Post-Baby:

How I Sometimes Dress Post-Baby:

Bag For Life.

It bothered me for a few days afterwards. In reality I think it was my defensive reaction that bothered me more than what she had said. I thought the only difference between my old style and my post-baby style was a few occasional stains and slightly more cumbersome accessories (try fitting a change of nappy into a clutch bag), but the truth was I now had a lot less time to worry about what to wear most days, which was probably a good thing. One less thing to worry about. And I now had the best accessory of them all – my sweet little boy.

How to know if you dress like a mum:

- You don't consider buying anything marked 'hand wash only'. And the few pre-baby things in your wardrobe that have this label end up at the bottom of the laundry basket for months (until your own mum offers to wash them).
- Ankle boots with a small block heel are your 'going out shoes'. Yes, you still have a few pairs of heels, but they make you angry after ten minutes of wearing them, and it's simply not worth it.
- You've kept a few pairs of those massive maternity pants at the bottom of your knicker drawer, and some days, they seem like they might be a good option.
- You now consider maxi dresses to be formal wear.
- The very idea of wearing white clothes makes you laugh hysterically.
- You start wearing baseball caps instead of going to the hairdresser.
- You long to wear all your nice jewellery again, but can only do it when there are no small people to yank it out of your ears/scratch/possibly choke on it.

NO-GO ZONES

ONE OF THE BIGGEST adjustments of parenthood comes long after the baby does; OK, so there are endless daily adjustments until your kids are 18 (translation: until you're dead), but there is one in particular that you may not have considered until you try to get back to your normal life. Just because a baby is now a permanent part of your life doesn't mean everyone else will want him or her as part of theirs. There are plenty of things now off-limits to you with a baby in tow, and most you will have anticipated: nightclubs, long weekend brunches, lie ins, and that sort of thing. But then there are all the ones you hadn't considered: many train stations (just try getting around London on the Tube with a buggy and you'll soon lose the will to live), some parts of your own town or city (there's really no excuse for the majority of places not to be accessible these days), and Your Mate's Wedding.

'What?', I hear you cry? 'Not my mate. She understands how much we love our babies and there's no WAY she'd plan her wedding and exclude them.' Well brace yourself, because chances are she has.

I have lost count of the angry parents I've heard over the years discussing how a family member or friend is 'selfishly' having a no-kids wedding or party. I used to mumble in agreement, when secretly I wondered why they wouldn't be glad of the enforced night off. Also, it was someone else's wedding and maybe they didn't want to have to worry about booking a clown and some kind of nuggets for dinner on top of everything else.

My husband and I had a no-kids wedding, and initially, he was horrified by the idea. But our venue wasn't child friendly, we were planning a late-night event, and it was abroad. In the end he was glad I'd insisted on it as all of our friends were tipsy and dancing in their bare feet at 4 a.m. thanking us for taking the decision out of their hands. Of course, however, not all of them were, and some didn't come presumably because of the 'thou shalt not bring babies' edict. But hey – our wedding, our choice. Well, our wedding, my choice, truth be told.

Since having my own baby, I understand the tricky logistics of organising babysitters for an event like a wedding, and when Tom was really small, I just turned most invites down. But even now, I don't understand the unique umbrage that some parents seem to take at their offspring being excluded. Suck it up, people. Suck it up or don't go.

Less easy to separate are other venues and events. Bars and many restaurants have a 'no kids after 6 p.m.'-type policy, which seems clear and fair, but it's the daytime places that aren't always so simple to navigate. Gone are the days of our grandparents, when mums stayed at home apart from a trip to pick up the meat for the week with the giant-wheeled pram. We are ladies who lunch, mums who munch (that sounds wrong) – walk down any high street during the daytime and you'll see the buggies lined up outside coffee shops like motorbikes outside a Hells Angels bar. And with this relatively new trend came the slew of cafés and other establishments who decided that children were not welcome. Yes, they banned the buggies ...

In certain cases, I wondered if the business owners were insane and if they knew who their demographic was at all. If you have the space and are attracting the lucrative mummy market, why not embrace it? Don't underestimate the parent pound.

I remember that a few years ago a chichi restaurant in Dublin 4 let it be known that anyone with a baby would have to go elsewhere (as politely as is ever possible when you are banning tiny people who are the centre of the person who's footing the bill's universe). Despite the inevitable uproar, however, I agreed with their decision. Mums and babies weren't their demographic. It was a small, pokey, overpriced place frequented by bankers, and to be honest, I wondered why they ever had to implement that rule in the first place as I was at a loss why any parent with a baby in tow would have wanted to go there.

It's a contentious issue, but I would rather go to a family-friendly location when I have my baby with me than a bar or restaurant where my money's not wanted and we will feel in the way. It's not discrimination – it's the reason there are family-friendly places at all. When I have a babysitter and want a night out or have a work meeting, I'll go to one of the baby-free places and enjoy the peace of mind that comes with not having to keep one eye on a crazed mini-crawler. And possibly have a mojito at midday. But if I'm meeting another mum and baby for a coffee, give me a ball pit instead of an amuse-bouche any day.

Just as I respect anyone choosing to make their business/party/wedding a child-free affair, equally I expect the person making that decision to respect the fact that sometimes, as a direct result of that ruling, I may have to stay away. It may sound obvious, but when Tom was small, I was invited to a 40th birthday party. I had no childcare so politely told them that unless I could bring the rug rat, I wouldn't be able to make it. I was told in no uncertain terms that no children were welcome. Fine, I couldn't go,

QED. However, suddenly I was chastised for not sorting childcare for this Terribly Important Party. Why couldn't I come? Why couldn't I just find a babysitter? Did I not have a neighbour who could watch him for a few hours? The questions were relentless.

Having kids doesn't mean you've lost yourself or your social life, but you may do less of what you used to do. And others need to understand this too. It's not personal, it's just a fact of life at this moment in time. I'm not having a covert dig at the no-babies brigade, I'm honestly not (I'm often one of them), but just asking that the respect works both ways. Maybe I genuinely couldn't get a babysitter or maybe I thought your party wasn't worth the extra cost.

I guess we'll never know.

THE ONE & ONLY

—

WHEN YOU GET to the point of motherhood where you're just getting on with things and you (for the most part) have your shit together, you might expect that you've had the baby, so you're done with the unsolicited questions on your fertility or broodiness and the intrusion on birth, breastfeeding and how fat you still are. Surely all the busybodies are getting on with their lives and there's nothing left to speculate on, is there?

Cue the 'uh-uh' klaxon from *Family Fortunes*. WRONG! I'd forgotten about the cardinal sin of daring to have only one child.

'You're not going to leave him as an only child are you?'

'Because of your age, you know you'd better have another one quickly?'

The ubiquitous 'only child discussions' will be familiar territory to any parent of one. People are terribly preoccupied with women and their wombs. They pity those who can't have children, cast aspersions on the ones who have too many, and shake their heads at those who don't want any at all. We can't win. And then there are women like me, who have a baby, and once the first year has passed, are bombarded with fabricated facts about solo kids:

'Only children are very introverted.' (Actually, it's the opposite.)

'Having a sibling makes them less selfish.' (The woman spouting this gem didn't realise the irony of her own children standing behind her as we spoke, almost killing each other over the last Tangfastic sweet in the bag. Schadenfreude, lady. You have selfish kids.)

'He'll be very alone when you die.' (WTF?! I hope he will have lots of friends, maybe a family and a lovely life all of his own, but cheers for that.)

I have heard them all: my son will be self-centred, lonely, spoiled, aggressive, bossy, friendless and possibly a psychopath. Seriously, someone said 'psychopath' about my tiny, smiley, happy baby.

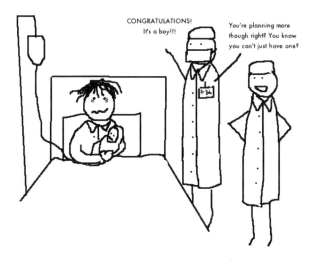

I have news for all of you only-child skeptics; the one-baby family is no longer the exception. It is more common than ever and all the long-held myths about only children have been debunked – only children are not socially inept; they are self-reliant and independent. They make strong friendships and often benefit from the additional time their parents or grandparents can afford them. A quick Google of famous only children throws up all sorts of non-psychopathic names: John Lennon,

Condoleezza Rice, Iris Murdoch, Lance Armstrong (shit, can we strike him from the list?). Hell, Harry Potter was an only child in fiction AND in real life.

That's not to say only children are better off without siblings (I'm not starting that fire) but let's not project our own ideals of what a family should be onto our kids. If you were one of two, three, four or more, then you might think that is the ultimate family unit. But every child will only know the dynamic they are born into - that will be their 'normal'. Good parenting is the important common denominator in a family, whether you have one child or ten. And if you do have ten, well, come here till we all judge you.

THE PARTNER

REMEMBER THE GOLDEN DAYS when it was just you and your partner? Your other half, your bae, your soulmate? Remember the fun you used to have before the arguments over money, where to live, taking the bins out, schools, in-laws (etc. *ad infinitum*)? Of course neither of you would swap your beautiful children for anything (this is rhetorical - please don't write lists of things you would in fact swap your children for), but there's no denying that Mummy and Daddy's relationship will move down the list of priorities when kids appear on the scene. Hell, it may even fall below taking the bins out. We know we have to make time for each other, but it's damn hard and on most days, there simply isn't any time left.

We focus a lot on what mums go through, but it's not easy for men either; they are often derided for not having gone through the labour pains, and expected to step into a role they were as unprepared for as we were for motherhood. There are times they will feel they are doing everything wrong, yet don't know what the right thing is. They will be as disconcerted as everyone else in the house by the madness that comes with a new baby, but will often be the ones expected to hold it all together - sometimes from the confines of the spare room.

There are a few conversations you will hear regularly between a group of new or not-so-new mums. These include (but are not limited to): breastfeeding highs and lows, exhaustion, baby's weight, mummy's weight, sleep patterns, baby shite, baby vomit ... the list goes on. But once the madness of life with a newborn settles into something resembling a routine, and you're just getting on with it all, there is one question that everyone really wants to know the answer to: when did you get back in the saddle?

Sex with your partner after having a baby might not be something you bring up with just anyone, but open a bottle of wine (or four) with a group of close pals, and the answers will make you feel more normal than you could ever have hoped for.

A friend of mine once told me that she begged her doctor to tell her husband at her six-week check-up that she really shouldn't have sex for at least six months, possibly even up to a year. He met her halfway and when her husband asked the question, he was non-committal with his answer, mumbling something about every woman being different and to take the lead from her. She said she felt slightly guilty when she saw her husband's crestfallen face but after another week of barely any sleep, she got over it pretty quickly.

I opened this can of worms with a group of mum pals and was amazed by how frank they all were. In a country not renowned for our openness about sex, they were delighted to share their stories and compare them with everyone else's - mainly to find out if their relationship was 'normal'.

'I didn't let him near me for six months,' one said.

'That's terrible! The poor guy! I felt bad so I made sure I gave him a least a fiddle after six weeks,' said another.

'You felt bad? I had fourth degree tearing! The only person feeling bad in my house was me - no way that bollix was going near me until I said so.'

'It took me ten months,' threw in another.

There were many shared stories about pretending to be asleep, bringing baby into the bed and moving husbands out of it for practical reasons (but then keeping that arrangement for months on end), and the more physical side – it wasn't always the tiredness that put women off the idea of sex, but often also body hang ups: stretch marks, scarring and sagging.

The words 'maintenance sex' were bandied about a lot, a term coined to mean the kind of sex you have out of a sense of duty rather than a genuine desire in a relationship. This may sound terribly depressing, and as women, this concept goes against everything we are told about love and consent, but in this hazy, post-baby world, it's not that simple. Sex and intimacy are important – they are what differentiates a relationship from other friendships and connections – but it is unrealistic to expect libidos to be equal at all times.

The general consensus was that maintenance sex was indeed a good thing. As one of my keen contributor friends said, 'Actually, when I do make myself do it, I end up enjoying it, and he always does more housework than usual the next day, so it's well worth it.'

'Jesus,' said another, 'Our kitchen needs to be painted. What would I have to do to get him to do that?'

I won't tell you the answer we came up with, but let's just say her whole house was newly painted the next time we saw her.

It's not all about sex of course, but keeping the friendship and communication going, which is where the twenty-first-century concept of date nights comes in to play. Date nights are great in theory and magazine articles with stock photos of attractive couples playing footsie under tables in expensive restaurants, but the very thought of them can strike fear into the heart of many a tired parent. Some people find them contrived, too much pressure or overly expensive (add the price of a babysitter on to a basic evening out and your early bird and cinema trip costs what you used to spend on a modest weekend away). You can't force people into having a nice time just because you call it 'date night'. And just how much effort do you have to make? Do you have to match your underwear? Do you have to put out after date night? Gah! We hate date night!

We all know relationships need to be nurtured. You are together by choice, and that choice must be cared for if it is to stay made. Having a baby doesn't always bring couples closer together - quite the opposite: it can tear them apart (which is why the concept of a band-aid baby is never, ever a good one). I have seen the happiest couples become chippy and distant with each other. The 'he's useless' comments about a partner who never gets anything right anymore, the eye rolls, the huffing and snapping on both sides. The tiredness and routine that come with having children, and the inalienable truth that the majority of work in the home is still done by mums can all build a slow but steady resentment.

One mum told me they couldn't justify the expense of date nights, but she said that instead, her husband and her made sure at least once a week all the kids were put to bed early and they had dinner and an evening where 'we agree to just be really nice to each other no matter what has happened that week, and ask the other person how they are. It works for us.' Another said her and her husband watch box sets together, which seems to be the new date night for many couples (let's be honest – box sets are essentially the glue that holds many marriages together).

So don't call it 'date night' if that grates, but do it in some shape or form. Spending time alone with your partner might just remind you of why you decided to have babies with them in the first place. Seeing them interact with other people at a party often shows you how other people view them, showing the good that maybe you lost sight of after surviving on three hours' sleep for so long. Watching others laugh in your partner's company might trigger the lovely memories of when you were laughing too, instead of rolling your eyes at how he has dressed the toddler or fed the kids pizza three times a day when you were away.

And if you still can't find any of the good stuff, then buy lots and lots of box sets.

CO-SLEEPING

—

I KNEW NOTHING about co-sleeping before I had a baby (frankly, it would have been weird as hell if I did). But whilst I was pregnant countless people asked me what my plans were vis-à-vis the baby's sleeping arrangements. I'd stare at them blankly and mutter something about a Moses basket and then moving him to a cot as soon as humanly possible. I was told about co-sleeping baskets, clever fold-out-and-attach systems, and other contraptions I still can't remember the names of.

The co-sleeping started out of pure practicality. I was exhausted, our room was in a loft conversion, and the thought of traipsing up and down narrow stairs at 4 a.m. was not appealing. When people asked, that's what I'd say.

'It's for convenience.'

'We make sure it's safe.'

'It's much easier for feeding.'

All the sensible, functional reasons. But fast forward nearly two years and it probably would have made sense for him to be in his own room, and he occasionally was, but more often than not, he ended up back in the big bed. I tried to justify it any which way I could. Then a woman I barely knew said to me, 'But isn't it lovely?'

REASONS YOU GIVE FOR CO-SLEEPING:

REASONS YOU REALLY CO-SLEEP:

- For the convenience
- Ease of feeding
- It's biologically appropriate
- Better for emotional development

It's just so snuggly and lovely...

And suddenly all the justification and explaining ceased to matter. That was the truth of it. It was indeed lovely. No one had ever said that to me before, but snuggling up beside this tiny, sweet-smelling, squishy little bundle was really lovely.

So I forgot about the excuses, explanations and rationale and just enjoyed it for what it was. I no longer felt the need to explain myself to anyone. I know that one day he won't be so tiny anymore and he will have his own room in a different house altogether. Maybe even in a different country (I feel slightly sick at that thought). I began to ignore all of the warnings about how I was making a rod for my own back and would have a hell of a time getting him into a routine. I decided early on in my parenting odyssey that if I were creating problems out of good intentions, then they'd be mine to fix. Admittedly as he got bigger, the headbutts started to hurt more and one morning he kicked me so hard in the face that my nose began to pump blood. But just as with the problems, the broken teeth will be mine to fix too.

FINDING YOUR STRIDE

COPING

ͨ෩

FINDING YOUR STRIDE in parenthood is a lovely feeling. Chances are you don't see it coming, or even know exactly when it happened, but you find yourself doing or saying something that might previously have seemed incomprehensible, and realise that you're actually quite good at this. Or at least you're not messing up all of the time. And that it's wonderful. Of course, finding your stride doesn't mean that everything suddenly becomes easy - ha! As if!

Some things change forever that you would prefer not to change. Your relationship will never be what it once was, but hopefully it will be richer (not literally - kids will bleed you dry) and transformed. You will never get entirely used to being exhausted, but you will adjust to it, and you will accept that coping is subjective. To quote my favourite columnist on the planet, Mary Schmich:

'Sometimes you are ahead, sometimes you are behind, but the race is long, and in the end, it's only with yourself.'

You know what's worse than the days that go wrong as a parent? The ones that almost go right. When you are so close to perfect parenting you can almost smell the baby-raising guru Gina Ford, but at the last minute it all falls apart. These days are the worst because you have been lulled into a false sense of security. You get smug and sloppy; like a serial killer who gets cocky and then makes a mistake.

As a mum, I have come to accept that there will be days when I don't cope well at all. Days when the kids are late for school, clothes are dirty, dishes hover precariously two feet above the sink waterline, showers are unwittingly missed, dinner comes under the heading of 'frozen foods' and everyone in the house goes to bed without brushing their teeth. But I have also come to accept that, actually, this is coping, it's just that there is a spectrum along which all of us will rally from one day to the next.

At one end of the Parental Coping Spectrum (PCS) is 'acing it': when we have those (admittedly rare for some of us) days when everything falls into place and gets done, not just satisfactorily, but brilliantly. You become one of those superwomen who you usually mutter a begrudging 'goodmorningpaula*' to through gritted teeth at the school gates. (*Name made up entirely at random. No Paulas were offended in the making of this book.) The one who's on time, looks great, has a three-tier stand of cupcakes for the charity bake sale in one hand, and her gym kit and idea-for-new-business folder under the other (NB: this person doesn't actually exist). Then the house gets cleaned, washing done (and ironed if you are off-the-scale acing it or a psychopath), emails replied to, bills paid, dog walked, or maybe a day's work outside the home is done (complete with making everyone laugh during a meeting and you see in your colleagues' eyes that they are in awe of how you do it all), TV license renewed, dinner prepped, and suddenly you find there's still time for a glass of wine and a bit of a box set after the kids go to bed.

At the other end of the PCS is 'shell of a human being'. I don't think I need to go into too much detail about these days, because no one wants to be reminded of them. These days of barely coping make Fortitude look like a pleasant place for a weekend away, and make the most miserable *EastEnders* Christmas special seem aspirational. None of us want to wish time away, but on these days, the hours can't pass quickly enough.

I remember I used to visit a friend years ago (long before babies were a part of my life) who was the most together person I knew. She had three kids quite young, was always organised and still managed to invite her old college pals (of whom I was one) over for dinner once in a while. We only had ourselves to look after and could barely do that, spending our lives in a tornado of drinks at lunchtime, hangovers, kissing inappropriate men and worrying about our careers. We would often leave her house after dinner, go to the pub on the way home, and discuss how we could never cope with a family the way she did. Ten years later and all of us now have kids (but we still agree she still has her shit together more than any of us).

But one day I called over to her and she was particularly stressed. Her husband was away and they'd argued before he left, her eldest was screaming for help with homework, her youngest was vomiting into the toilet (but missing the bowl) and the middle one was treading dog poo into the carpet. Yet STILL she held it together. She joked saying she'd fix us both a drink and went to the freezer to get some ice. Alas, there was none and that's when it happened. She flipped. I mean went ballistic. It was such a massive overreaction to something so unimportant, especially given the rest of the chaos in the house.

Fast forward a few years and now I get it. I call it 'the straw that breaks the mama's back'. It's the cumulative effect of lots and lots of small things, resulting in a monumental overreaction to something seemingly trivial. Of course, sometimes it's not something trivial, but many times it is.

And it's not surprising. Take the most über-organised, upbeat person in the world; add a flurry of tiny people with no regard for breakables or personal safety, throw in a level of sleep deprivation that under any other circumstances would trigger a UN human rights investigation, garnish with a sprinkling of judgment from the outside world and it's no wonder that we occasionally snap. In my case, the straw has been a slice of burnt toast and once when I was really, really exhausted, it was someone buying the wrong type of milk. Immaterial, utterly unimportant stuff in the grand scheme of things, but sometimes you just need to scream about something.

Most mothers operate at 100 per cent capacity all of the time, 24 hours a day, 7 days a week. If any other job required such dedication, not only would it lead to a tribunal of some sort, but it would be understandable that someone would periodically snap and kick over the water cooler.

So what can we do about it? Practice mindfulness or attend therapy? Spend your life in a terrible cycle of apologising and beating yourself up? Maybe, if you can find the time for any of that. But if you accept that it might happen from time to time, know that those who love you will get over it, give yourself a break and move on, you'll find it's over as soon as it's begun. That is, unless you're my pal whose straw was dropping a yoghurt in the supermarket. The staff were lovely about it, but she cried and cried as if every single person she knew had just died.

She, too, got over it; but she had to find a new supermarket.

Thankfully, for the most part, we sit in the middle of the spectrum, our days dictated by routine and peppered with small triumphs and minor disasters. At the start of motherhood, I naively planned for every day to be at the 'acing it' end of the scale, but the sooner you accept that that doesn't happen (outside of Gwyneth Paltrow's ten-bedroom, self-cleaning house), the happier you will be. Now I embrace the barely coping days. I remind myself that tomorrow will be better, and that there's still plenty to love about today no matter how exhausting or chaotic. Because even on the days where life feels like walking through treacle, we need to congratulate ourselves on a job well done.

THE TIREDNESS

I DON'T THINK I need to tell any parent about tiredness. We get bored of being warned about it by exhausted parent friends before we even have kids (the ones who tell us to sleep now while we can). Then we get pissed off with well-meaning folk asking us no end of questions related to sleep after a baby arrives. 'Is he sleeping? Are you sleeping? Is Dad sleeping? Are the other kids sleeping? IS ANYONE SLEEPING?' We get it. Babies sleep in cycles of only a couple of hours. They wake up during the night. Many of them take years to settle into a routine ... blah blah blah. We always knew this, we just didn't have to worry about it before.

But after a year or so, I had a new beef with tiredness. I realised that it got in the way of absolutely everything.

Maybe I should have expected this, but I thought that once the newborn phase was over and baby started going to bed at a reasonable hour, I'd be amazed at how having a couple of hours to myself in the evenings would be a lifeline. I wasn't expecting miracles (see above: we always knew this), and I wasn't planning to resume my pre-baby social life, but I was hoping to just get a small bit of time to myself. But I didn't because I was too damn tired.

Once all the humdrum, daily grind stuff was done, I'd think 'Huzzah! Half an hour to do something for me!' and would sit down to read a paper, but only get through four lines before I started to drift. I tried to catch up on all the brilliant telly I'd missed and within minutes, my head was lolling. I checked emails, but my brain missed massive chunks of important information and I had to re-read them a hundred times. My sister offered to babysit, I went out for dinner with friends, and by 8.30 p.m., I willed the kitchen to catch fire so they'd have to evacuate the restaurant and I could go home because I was so knackered. My husband and I went away on a frankly magnificent three-night, baby-free break when our little guy was about 16 months old. We planned dinners, walks, movies and cocktails, but by about 9 p.m. every night my eyelids felt like someone had attached fishing weights to them. Even when I just said, sod it, this is my life now, and went to bed at 9 p.m. to read, I managed half a page and would awake four hours later to a cry on the baby monitor and the book stuck to my face, still on the same page.

Tiredness thwarted everything.

The Plan When Baby Goes To Bed:

HOORAY!
Now I can
tidy up,
check emails,
shave my legs,
watch telly...

The Reality When Baby Goes To Bed:

Zzzzzzzz

Some friends understood and others didn't. I had a chat with a woman who was happily child-free as her 40th birthday approached, and was planning a big party. She told me she wasn't inviting her oldest friend because she had a new baby, was always tired and would no doubt go home early. This stung, and I was glad not to be on her guest list, because new mums don't need to be told they're pooping the party.

We vow not to change once our babies arrive; we promise ourselves that we'll still be us, and still have time for our friends and the odd night out. But then we accept that we can't do it all – at least not all of the time, and certainly not with a newborn. Then I realised that her decision said more about her selfishness than her old friend/new mum's stamina. No new mum goes home early because she can't be arsed to stay out; chances are she's been up in the night with kids, had packed lunches to make, couldn't afford to be hungover, or might just have been completely exhausted. She may not have fundamentally changed, but her priorities have, and her tiredness levels reflect that. I also didn't get why it mattered so much to this woman if one person went home early (unless she was the only guest which maybe was the problem), but as a mum – and especially as a new first-time mum – you need people to just understand without the need for explanation or justification. She'll never know – her old pal might also have ended up being the last woman standing.

A couple of times a year, a few friends and I plan a night away, about which we are always disproportionately excited. It's only 24 hours, but the restorative powers of that one day are immeasurable (well, maybe not immeasurable, but let's just say they're significant). The best thing about them is that they are populated by all mums (bar one, but she's entirely made of empathy) so the pressure is off and the tiredness is accepted. Even though we are always determined to have a drink or two and enjoy our child-free time away, there is also an unspoken understanding that if someone wants a nap rather than another gin, there will be no judgment and no one will roll their eyes, tell you how dull you are, or worse, remind you 'how you've changed!' Of course we perpetually hold out hope that we'll stay out till 3 a.m., but then sometime around midnight, someone will remember that we've had twenty years of that and say, 'Oh, wouldn't it be lovely to be fresh for breakfast and actually enjoy it being cooked by someone else without little people hassling us?' (because it would be very bad form if that happened in a hotel).

Damn you, tiredness; what have you done to us?

THE
INEQUALITY

—

THERE IS always the odd occasion when a mum goes to town, takes the candle, burns it at both ends (and then melts the middle bit for good measure), and when this happens we are judged yet again, but at the other end of the scale.

If we're not being toweringly dull, we're being extraordinarily irresponsible. There's no more letting the side down when you become a mother. It's different for dads; from the wetting of the baby's head within days of the new arrival (can you imagine the criticism a group of mums doing the same in a pub would get?) to the nights out with the lads because they need to let off steam, dads can still get away with it. Not so for most mums. Once you are a mother, your only job is to be a short order cook, a milk machine and a mummy.

The inequality doesn't stop there. Mothers are judged for going back to work and for not going back to work. If we don't do it all, we're letting ourselves down, and if we do pull it off, we're showing off or letting our kids down. My generation is the first who was led to believe we could have it all. We could go to college, we could travel, build careers, get married (or not), have kids (or not), and do it all on a par with men. Glass ceiling? What glass ceiling?! We couldn't see it until we hit it so hard we ended up with concussion.

I've watched as my female friends and I tie ourselves up in knots trying to make everything work, and we have very few avenues of advice. I grew up in Ireland, a country where until 1973, women working in the public sector were prevented by law from going back to, or starting, work after they married, and it took some time after that for the numbers of women in the workplace to rise again. And even though the landscape has changed dramatically over the last 45 years, there is still a notable difference in the numbers of women with and without children in employment. We don't need the reasons why explained to us.

Anecdote-to-make-a-point-time: a friend of mine who has a 'big job' (as my own mum would say) in finance is the main earner in her family, so her husband is the primary contact given to the school in case of emergencies and her number is second. Yet every time without fail that someone has to be called, they call her, and when she asks why they didn't call her husband first, they say, 'Oh, we assumed it was a misprint.'

It's not men's fault, and most of us are lucky to be surrounded by supportive man-folk. I could write an entire book about the great imbalances that exist in the workplace and out of it, the gender pay gap, how we need more support with child care, the disparity in the treatment of mothers and fathers across the board, paternity vs maternity leave, flexible working hours and so on, but that's a different book entirely (and for the answers, please see Sweden). But for the sake of this discussion, all I can say is that the happiest women I know are the ones who accept that how much they can do is relative to nothing else but their own circumstances.

And so, there are some of us juggling work and a family, others who are child-free with great careers, some who have great careers and great child-minders, more who are stay-at-home mums, and others still who study at night with a plan to get back to work when the kids are gone (ha! In 40 years!), but the common denominator for happiness is not comparing, not judging and the acceptance of the things that are beyond our control. It all comes down to the old serenity prayer that wisdom is rooted in knowing the difference between the things that are within our power to change and those that aren't. But that's all getting a bit serious. Let's also remember the (possible) alternative wording:

'God grant me the serenity to know when I just need to get hammered and dance in a fountain.'

What many mums try to do to resolve the perennial go-back-to-work/do-not-go-back-to-work debate is to meet it halfway with the twenty-first-century option of working from home.

Surely this is the perfect solution? You can spend all that precious time with your baby whilst still keeping a career going, earning money and doing it all without worrying about power suits or brushing your hair!

WRONG.

Working from home with a baby or toddler is an unmitigated nightmare. I'm going to stick my neck out here and say that it is virtually impossible. If you work outside the home, you have to be gone by a certain time in the morning – no one's saying it's easy, but you do. Come hell, high water or toddler tantrum, you have to get your kids to school or childcare and once you do, they're not around to vomit on you or make unreasonable demands like wanting to be fed or played with. Not so with working from home. Working from home is like working in an office that is constantly under siege. Your working environment is perpetually like the first *Die Hard* movie (and they didn't get much work done there while Alan Rickman and his band of terrorists held them at gunpoint, did they?). Add to that in real life Bruce Willis* doesn't break in via an air vent and offer free childcare services (if only …). (*I've just realised that this is the second reference to Bruce Willis in this book. He's never far from my mind, truth be told.)

On an average day, I might have a column to write and a conference call, things I would have struck off the list before 10 a.m. without a second thought in my previous life. But these days, an attempt at a 'work from home day' looks a little like this:

- Get up (after four hours of broken sleep),
- get everyone breakfast,
- clean up breakfast detritus,
- stress over column being two days late already,

- dress baby,
- take baby to park (to assuage the guilt of inevitably dumping him in front of an iPad later),
- get home,
- prep lunch,
- try to take part in conference call whilst entertaining baby (ensuring webcam is off to avoid horrifying other participants),
- put baby down for nap,
- remember I haven't showered yet,
- jump in shower,
- sit down to work,
- disturbed by waking baby,
- get baby back up and change him again (there was a nappy leak so also change sheets),
- give baby lunch,
- clean lunch off walls,
- try to write a few words whilst baby cries and pulls at legs,
- feel guilty,
- panic over not having anything in for dinner for rest of family,
- try to force baby to take second nap unsuccessfully,
- wish someone would force you to take a nap,
- check emails and placate editors hounding for three overdue columns,

- notice house hasn't been tidied in two weeks,
- panic/feel guilty again,
- wonder why you have a pain in your side and realise you've needed a wee for the last hour,
- stick baby in front of iPad,
- go for wee,
- scribble a few more words,
- prep dinner,
- moan to family over dinner about how little work you got done today,
- put baby to bed,
- turn to wine,
- resent wine for not helping,
- sit down to finish work,
- realise it's 10 p.m. and you're exhausted and a bit tipsy,
- cry,
- your crying wakes up baby,
- settle baby,
- give up on day,
- go to bed,
- get up three times during the night,
- start all over again.

On the occasions when I have to leave the house for work, and my husband or mum take the baby, it is infinitely easier. More than that, the freedom that comes with it makes work feel like a break (any mum who, like me, has spent 24/7 with their kids will know the lightness of being that comes from occasionally, just occasionally being without them). So as grateful as I am to have built up a career that allows me - on paper - to work from home, I have accepted that the 'working from home' thing may well be an oxymoron.

I know it won't be forever, realistically I may only have one baby, and so I accept it for what it is. I know that the day will come when he trots off to school on his own, I can go to work hassle- and guilt-free, and I will pine for the days when it was just me, him and a long list of work that never got done.

HAVE CHILD, WILL TRAVEL

—

THERE SHOULD BE AWARDS handed out to mothers and fathers for various achievements throughout parenthood; as if we were in an adult version of Brownies or Cub Scouts, but without the necessity for unflattering uniforms or toggles.

'Congratulations! You've earned your changed-a-nappy-on-a-moving-bus badge!'

'Well done! Here's your mopped-up-vomit-and-changed-the-sheets-at-3 a.m. badge!'

'Best wishes to you! You've just got your made-it-out-of-the-supermarket-after-a-toddler-tantrum badge!'

You get the idea. One of the many milestones parents have to face sooner or later is travelling with children. It might be packing them all up in a car to visit grandma, or maybe if you're lucky it's going on a lovely holiday somewhere, but the thought of travelling further than school or the supermarket with kids in tow is overwhelming for some people.

Like every other aspect of parenthood, once you do it and no one dies, you realise it isn't remotely as bad as you'd feared. I had to travel a lot when Tom was a baby and unfortunately had to do it all solo. When I hear people whinging about having to fly with a baby when their partner is with them, I scoff. You have it easy! You have two sets of hands and can go to the toilet if you need to.

If you've never flown solo with a baby and would like to know what it's like, just put an angry cat into one of those sturdy plastic 'bags for life', and try and ride a bicycle around a busy roundabout. Full of impatient motorists. At rush hour.

My first solo flight with Tom was when he was just eight weeks old, and I was terrified. But we got through it, we both made it out alive, no strangers were vomited on, Tom was amazing and it lulled me into a false sense of security. In the two years that followed, we made over fifty solo flights with varying degrees of success.

Since having a baby, I see all forms of transport in newly challenging ways. Less than a quarter of underground stations in London have step-free access. If a bus pulls up and there are already two buggies on board, you have to wait for the next one. Trying to get anywhere on public transport during rush hour elicits the kind of eye rolling usually reserved for accordion players, as you apologise profusely to everyone who glances and huffs at you and your buggy taking up the space of two people. Trust me folks, if buggy owners didn't have to be somewhere at the same time as you, they wouldn't be out at peak times. They don't do it just to piss other commuters off. But public transport is a walk in the park in comparison to flying. Well, not all flights, but when a flight goes bad, it can go into Adam Sandler movie territory.

I learned early on to be organised with military detail. Ten minutes before boarding, there is a nappy change for the little guy and a wee for me (it's impossible to go for a wee on a plane with a baby unless you ask a stranger to hold him/her). But even a simple wee isn't straightforward when travelling solo. The majority of baby changing rooms don't have a toilet. I almost weed in the sink once, but had visions of it falling off the wall and me having to justify myself to airport security. Not a reason for which I'd like to be banned for life from Heathrow. (NB: this is a massive oversight, airport-facility-design-people, but kudos to Dublin Airport for pulling it off. And now I've just read that sentence back and realised how utterly depressing it is that my life has gone from airport bars to airport toilets.)

Once that caper is over, it is time to run the gauntlet of the priority queue. Despite the ground staff clearly inviting anyone travelling with infants to come forward first, you'd swear I had wronged every person in the queue judging by the looks I get as I manoeuvre to the front. No one seems to recognise that there is a logic to letting us on first, it's as if they think they might miss out on something wonderful and due to them if I reach the plane door first. The fancy-pants card holders and business commuters are the worst. Their faces and reactions tell me we have no right to be on a plane at all. 'Sure, wouldn't the bus and ferry be a better combo for you and that contraption, missy?', their supercilious sneers imply.

Once on a flight, I was sitting beside a woman who told me without a hint of irony or humour that she was 'allergic to babies'. I get angry thinking about her now, as I have since had a hundred conversations in my head about what I should have said to her, but it was relatively early on in my travel training, and there is something about being a new mum that makes you feel a bit vulnerable. It's what makes you apologise for everything – asking for help with stairs, getting in people's way, or taking up more than your own footprint on a train. I stopped being apologetic pretty quickly, but at this point I wasn't quite there yet. Plus this woman was horrendous. She spent the flight huffing about the chances of her expensive hat getting crushed in the overhead locker, and sighing loudly in my direction every time Tom moved a muscle. He slept for the entire flight, was an angel and when he woke up as we were landing, reached out and touched her arm, I apologised (yet again) and she said, 'You're fine. Do you know why you're fine? Because he was quiet.'

I smiled defeatedly, but what I wanted to say (and am saying now in the unlikely hope that she'll read this one day) was:

'What the fuck? I paid the same as you for my seat - actually, I paid more to carry my baby on my lap (I'm surprised you didn't book a separate seat for your fucking hat, by the way) and I had as much right to be on that plane as you. I realise you don't like babies and that's fine. There are plenty of offices, bars, restaurants and holidays you can enjoy child free, but I'm afraid you can't make them disappear from everyday life. Oh, and I caught a glimpse of your hat as you got off the plane. It was hideous and will make you look like an angry emu.'

I know she'll never read it, but I feel better now. A friend suggested that maybe this woman couldn't have children and found it painful; trust me, that wasn't her story. Not every woman wants to have children and that's fine. I honestly believe it's important for many reasons for some women to not want to have children; for a long time I thought I might be one of them (at 4 a.m. some mornings I still am). But even when I had those thoughts, I had admiration and empathy for mothers. Yes, I will admit my heart often sank when I saw a woman with a baby take the seat beside me on a plane (I was usually hungover and looking forward to a nap), but I could usually see the mild fear in her eyes, and even if the baby did cry for the entire flight, it's a BABY, not a drunk stag party. Even if you don't have one, you were once one, and isn't it great that we live in a world where mums and babies can get on a plane in the first place?

Even before I had a child, I understood the people who said, 'You don't really understand until you become a parent.' I never found that patronising as some people do.

I got it. The same way you can't really explain grief, or love, or teenage angst to someone with no experience of them.

Of course there are always lovely people too. Helpful cabin crew who offer a hand. The gent who smiled and carried my bag for me, telling me he has two at home. The woman who turned around as Tom wailed (and just before I started to cry) and told me not to worry about the noise, sure, wasn't he only a baby and wasn't it only a short flight. I could have hugged those people.

In the early days of taking those flights, I would reach my destination, walk out of arrivals and honestly feel that I could take on the world.

Until I remembered I still had to catch a bus.

HOLIDAYS

ONCE YOU'VE MASTERED the art of travel, then you can go ANYWHERE! Right? If you're one of those lucky enough to have the time and finances to plan a holiday, do it! Holidays bring out the best in people. They are small windows of respite from the conveyor belt of ordinary life - with added cheap cocktails and beachwear. Remember when you would choose your holiday based on two factors alone? How much money you had and what you liked to do?

There are families who say that you can take kids anywhere, and I remember thinking that I'd be one of those mothers who goes trekking in Thailand with a baby on her back. But now, I can't imagine anything I'd like to do less.

The reality of motherhood for most women means that holidays are not breaks for mums at all. Yes, it's great to spend quality time with the whole family together away from work and the humdrum of home life, but when you have young children, the humdrum of home life tends to be packed alongside the suncream and travel adapters.

A break from work is a wonderful thing, but if your work is in the home, then unless you can afford an all-inclusive resort somewhere, someone still has to do the cooking, the cleaning, the getting up in the night and the wiping of bottoms – assuming you have children in nappies (or are into very niche adult holidays …)

A friend confessed to me: 'For the last three years we have gone on camping holidays to France. I try and relax and I love seeing my husband unwind and my kids have a blast, but in all truth, it isn't a holiday for me at all. First, there's the unique fear that only comes from travelling with three kids under eight, and when we get there, I still have to do everything I do at home just in a more confined space. I'm always wrecked when we get home, but I see these times as making memories for the kids, not a relaxing break for me.'

And therein lies the truth for many mums on holiday. Yes, you can try and cook simple stuff or eat out if it's an option, bring enough clothes to avoid washing every day, and not feel guilty of availing of the kids' club whilst you lie on a sun lounger, but for many, it's just the same chores done in a different place with a foreign brand of washing powder.

Most parents who are fortunate enough to be able to afford a holiday wouldn't admit to this, and they know that even if it isn't necessarily a holiday for them, if they had to choose between a kid-free luxury spa vacation or a down and dirty, sand-in-your-bed family holiday, the latter would win every time.

Well, most of the time.

Then there are those great multi-annual events that become the World's Biggest Misnomers when kids arrive: bank holidays. In my pre-baby, full-time working life, they would fill me with joy for weeks in advance. Three-day weekend! Or for the ones that would fall over Easter – four! (Once you made sure to stock up on a few bottles of wine for Good Friday).

Bank holidays meant lie ins followed by brunches that turned into entire days in beer gardens, and the unique bliss that only comes from being up late and eating takeaway on a Sunday night safe in the knowledge that Monday doesn't count this week. Oh yes, there really is something truly magical about bank holidays. Or rather, was.

I noticed years ago how my friends with kids would roll their eyes, 'Oh God, it's a bank holiday and I don't know what to do with the kids,' they'd moan. 'And the weather forecast is bad.'

Lighten up! It's a bank holiday, I'd think. And if the weather is bad then you just sit inside the pub rather than outside.

Oh how naive I was, and what I'd give for just one of those halcyon triple-Saturdays now.

Because now, of course, I get it. I see the scores of parents queuing up bleary eyed outside the zoo before it even opens, in parks, at the cinema, at city farms and at other places I didn't even know existed before I had a baby. I know because I've joined their ranks. Desperate to get somewhere before the crowds (and, sure, aren't kids all up at 6.30 a.m. on a bank holiday Monday anyway?), packing nappies, snacks, sippy cups and a range of jackets for the Irish weather.

Bank holidays went from being a mini-break to an endurance test. Yes, you'll find you might still do the occasional pub lunch out, but now you have to find the family-friendly places with kiddie meals, changing tables, soft play areas and plenty of parking. Someone has to drive, so drinking is out anyway, and even if you could, it would be warm by the time you got to drink it as you'll spend half the afternoon following the random child who keeps knocking yours off the swing around the playground. Then it's back in the car and hitting the rush hour bank holiday traffic home with restless kids who need poo poos and such.

Then there are those families who brave Ikea on a bank holiday ... they've lost me already.

Once you have a family, not unlike with charity, holidays should begin at home. It's OK to accept offers of help from grandparents, or to remind our other halves that even one night off without actually going anywhere can be as restful as a five-star break (well, not quite, we'd still like a five-star break).

THE
OCCASIONS

AS THE MOTHERHOOD JOURNEY continues, you keep crossing new bridges as and when you come to them. You do what comes naturally and what feels right, and then you see other people doing things differently, tie yourself up in knots, and wonder if you are making a hames of it all. Then one day, you stop giving a shit, and that's a day worth celebrating in itself.

It's often the other days worth celebrating that illustrate the difference between styles of parenting. Birthdays, Christmases, Easters, Halloween. Some parents seem to believe that how much you spend or how much effort you make is directly proportional to how much you love your child.

On Tom's first birthday, it had never occurred to me to make a massive deal outside of our family, spend a fortune and shout it from the rooftops. In my head, I wanted to write it across the sky in fireworks and take out a full page ad in *The Times*, but in reality, I bought a Gruffalo cake and a number '1' candle.

But (as is the way with every first baby milestone), it was only when the comments started coming that I was made to feel I had done something wrong.

'He's one? Gosh, you kept that quiet, didn't you?' (Um, not really. It was 12 months after I told everyone I'd had a baby.)

'Oh, I remember our Billy's first birthday. We got caterers in.' (Bugger. I made a one pot and invited the grandparents.)

'Did you get him a special gift?' (No. He's one. I have enough years ahead when he'll demand special gifts. Why would I spend a fortune when he finds tissue paper pant-wettingly exciting?)

'Did you hire a professional photographer?' (No. No I didn't, because I'M NOT INSANE!)

'Have you heard that boxer Amir Khan spent £100,000 on his daughter's second birthday?' (Good for him. The gobshite.)

It wasn't just one person who passed remarks about our low-key celebrations. There were several. And as a first timer to all this, for a split second I genuinely worried that I had made a grave mistake that would damage my son irreparably. Somewhere down the line, he would ask about his first birthday, and I would have to break the news to him that all I have are a few photos taken on an iPhone of him crying beside a cross-eyed, shop-bought Gruffalo cake.

And then, as had happened countless time over my first 12 months of motherhood, I checked myself. I came to my senses. I had done the right thing. We were talking about a tiny person who had only recently realised he had opposable thumbs. There would be enough times in the future when spending money would be a necessity: school trips, the new iPhone 15, bailing him out of jail ... it made no sense to spend a small fortune on a party at that stage. The first few birthdays of a child's life are really for parents, grandparents, older siblings and posterity. If you have time to make a cake yourself, great. If you want to put together a keepsake gift for the future, lovely. If you spend the cost of a modest wedding on someone who can just as easily be entertained by a shoelace in the belief that it's for the child, then you may need to rethink things.

And so I accepted the occasional invites to other people's children's first birthday parties graciously, brought gifts, drank the prosecco, enjoyed the catered food, tried to avoid the over-enthusiastic photographer with the Instagram selfie frame, and didn't resent them or envy them (well, I was kind of irritated by the Instagram selfie frame), but never once regretted my decision to keep it small.

What can be even more difficult to navigate than birthdays is Christmas. Birthdays can slip under the radar without too much fanfare if you're careful, but there's no avoiding the potential for Christmas gift-shaming.

For the sake of full disclosure, I'm about as Christmassy a person as you could meet, without crossing over into Christm-ass-hole territory (you know what I'm talking about – novelty jumpers that require batteries, 12 pubs of Christmas, etc.). At this point, I've had two December 25ths as a mum, and kept both of them simple. Why? Because Baby Tom was too young to get it!

'WHAT?!', I hear at least one person holler.

Of course I took photos of him in ludicrous pudding babygros, I bought all grandparents cute decorations with his face thereon, I even made him a Christmas comforter last year from the previous year's festive babygro (I can't believe I've confessed to that gem). So you see, I'm not a Grinch on any level. But until children have more of an awareness of the whole seasonal shebang, let's just admit that it's more for the grown-ups and there's no point in bankrupting yourself. There's nothing wrong with it being for the grown-ups – we need to make memories for ourselves too. Tom is the first grandchild on my side of the family, and seeing the unbridled joy he has brought into my parents' house is nothing short of extraordinary, but I am aware that he won't remember Christmases for a few years yet, and so while it's important for the rest of us to enjoy every moment, flying him to Lapland for the sake of a photo really isn't on my agenda.

You heard me. I met a woman who was bringing her two-year-old twins to Lapland last year (and no, she doesn't have older kids). Intrigued as to her motivation and the outcome, I had to find out via a third party how the trip went. The twins spent the entire 72 hours cold and terrified; one was nibbled by a reindeer and now won't go near any animal larger than a hamster, and the other was left with a pathological fear of men with white beards. The self-righteous me was quietly delighted.

I'm sure most of us are on the same page with this one. My usual disclaimer applies – if you want to go enormously over the top for the under-threes at Christmas, then by all means knock yourself out. But if you're already struggling to buy presents for your in-laws, then why add to your stress and January debt by spending a fortune on the tiny person who won't remember it?

I was asked numerous times in the run up to my first two Christmases as a mum if I brought Tom to see Santa or what I was buying him for Christmas, and the answer both years was no and nothing. Well, that was a lie; he had some new Christmas clothes and a rattle the first year, and a beanbag the second which was too big to wrap up. On Christmas morning, we let him play with some wrapping paper, shoved him into an empty box with a novelty turkey hat on for the obligatory photo, but not once did I feel guilty for not indulging him with things that he would have no interest in. Although I have just remembered that for his second Christmas, my husband bought him a remote control car; but I think we all knew who that was really for.

I can't wait for the Santa years, the list-writing, elves on shelves and teaching him my favourite carols. But until those years arrive, he can make do with wrapping paper.

But the gift and spending dilemmas don't end with your own decisions or even your own children. Once you join the mama club, and you and your new baby (especially the first) arrive home, the presents you receive may seem as numerous as the dirty nappies. I tried to take note of who sent what so as to be able to thank people, but in those early, hazy days, it's easy to forget another bunch of flowers or pack of gift-wrapped muslin cloths (apologies if any pals reading this sent a present that went un-thanked for. They were all gratefully appreciated. Except the pal who sent the rattle shaped remarkably like a penis - you know who you are). Friends with more than one child told me to embrace it as the presents lessen with each baby. One mate with five kids said she didn't receive so much as a single card for her fifth. Poor numero cinco (not the child's actual name).

So what are the rules or are there any? Often when a friend has a new baby, people will also get a gift for baby's first Christmas and first birthday, but where do you draw the line? Do you keep buying presents for friends' kids indefinitely? What if you've started - is it even possible to stop?

Unless it's a very good friend, family member or you're godparent to their child, buying gifts on an ongoing basis sets an awkward precedent; not only will it become increasingly difficult to stop, but they will feel the need to reciprocate with your kids and before you know it, everyone's buying gifts for 98 children at Christmas.

CHRISTMAS 2007

CHRISTMAS 2017

I can hear the shouts of 'Scrooooooge!' from some of you already, but I'm sure others are nodding in solidarity. I have an insanely generous (slash foolish) friend who started buying Christmas presents for everyone's babies when they were born. Then she didn't stop. I met her last December in a panic in TK Maxx, a trolley full of plastic toys I guarantee no one needed (or wanted). This year she said she is just going to get them all a selection box, but I know she'll cave at the last minute and buy up half the Argos catalogue in a blind panic.

Then I know other people who refuse to be guilted into subscribing to such extravagances. They buy a new baby a 'welcome to the world' gift, and after that, it's down to grandparents and Santa to bridge any gaps.

I decided to be brave. I agreed with friends that we wouldn't buy each other's kids presents, and that we'd use the money to go for lunch ourselves a few times a year. Most of them agreed. Of course there was one who was horrified by the suggestion so I had to pretend I was kidding and ran out to panic buy her kid a present. Because I can be an idiot like that; I'm great at being decisive and sensible until someone implies I'm mean, and then I can crumble like an abandoned rusk under a sofa. Next year I'll try again ...

BOOZE

A FEW YEARS AGO I unwittingly became a poster girl for 'women and drinking'. I hadn't intended to, but I made a documentary called *Merlot & Me* in which I openly discussed my own drinking in relation to new national statistics, and alongside other women who were candid about their own alcohol habits. Since then, I am repeatedly asked to comment any time a newspaper or talk show covers the subject, as if I either have:

A) a problem
B) all the answers

I don't have either.

Our generation's drinking habits are very different to those that came before. Sometime around the mid '90s, alcohol snuck out of the off-licences (it must have had its own keys cut and left under the cloak of darkness) and crept into the supermarkets. But even then, it stayed in the designated booze section of the shop, knowing its place. Then one day, when we were all looking the other way, it quietly moved itself into the main bits of the supermarket. Alcohol is smart, and worked out pretty quickly that women are still predominantly responsible for 'the big shop'. It then realised that a lot of these women are knackered mums and so wheedled its way into shiny displays at the end of the baby aisle. I hadn't noticed this before (as I would only ever use the baby aisle as a short cut to the mixers), but since becoming aware of it, I have lost count of the number of times I have seen a pyramid of Prosecco, stack of Sauvignon or sparkly stand of Chardonnay within burping distance of the baby wipes.

Alcohol is hunting us down, people.

Now I don't want to get all sanctimonious here, but there's no denying many of us make throwaway jokes about 'mummy juice' or 'wine o'clock' and read endless funny Facebook posts about wine. As someone who used to socialise around alcohol, I can't deny I sometimes miss going on those big nights out, but equally I know the hangover just isn't worth it anymore. Recently I admitted to a friend that I have days where I am literally counting the hours (and sometimes minutes) until it would be acceptable to fix a drink (NB: 11 a.m. is not it). I thought this was a dreadful confession and a worrying sign until she threw her head back, laughed and told me that I was far from alone. It turns out a lot of mums are also doing it, and it's what gets many of them through tougher days.

Why? I used to have a busy full-time job and didn't count the hours until I could have a drink. But here's the difference; when you're a stay-at-home parent, there is very little that is just for you anymore. Despite the joy that comes with this particular job, there can also be a monotony to it, and having something 'grown up' in your day that's just for you, or you and a friend, or you and your partner, is nice. I have read many people extolling the virtues of teetotalism – the clear head, the shiny skin, the slimmer tummy (I liked the sound of that) – so I cut out my seemingly regular evening drink completely for nearly six weeks to see how great I'd feel in the morning (I say nearly, as I did break it one night for a friend's leaving do. I'm not a total martyr to the cause). Aside from being relieved that I could do it, I didn't honestly feel less fuzzy headed in the mornings for it (it transpired it was the baby waking at 2/4/6 a.m. that was responsible for the fuzziness, not the drink).

An expert of some sort once told me that we shouldn't reward ourselves with alcohol. We should see things like a bath or taking a nice walk as rewards. But what mother has time for a bath? The truth is, 200 millilitres in a glass is easier than 40 litres in a bath (of water - please do not fill your baths with booze ...).

door bell

Be with you in a jiffy! I'm just restocking the medicine cabinet.

What is the answer to this seemingly perpetual - and quite Irish - conundrum? Motherhood aside, no one has ever really been able to give me a satisfactory answer to the age-old question of why many Irish people have a less than healthy attitude to booze. But in the short term, and in relation to this current stage of my life, I've learned a few things:

- No, looking forward to a drink doesn't make you an alcoholic.
- Yes, we probably should joke about it a bit less.
- No, it doesn't mean you're now a dullard if you sometimes need a drink to feel more like your old self.
- But yes, it might be a problem if you need ten.

In a nutshell, I'm talking about our old friend 'moderation'.

I probably enjoy alcohol more now – and in a better way – than I ever did. Things have moved on from the drinking to get drunk or Dutch courage of youth. Now I want to have a grown-up relationship with booze, not cut it out altogether.

I still have one drink most evenings, but I've started making sure I have at least a few nights off, if for no other reason than to know that I have the upper hand. I don't need anything else to feel guilty about.

NOT ALL KIDS ARE LOVELY

—

SINCE HAVING A BABY, there is no denying that I have become more of a 'baby person'. I empathise when I see a stressed mum, or hear a toddler raising the roof of a supermarket with their screams. I lean in to prams and buggies more than I used to (actually, I never used to), smile and ask how old/what are they called/how are they doing. Oh yes, I am much more child friendly than before.

But it doesn't mean I suddenly like all children. Children are people and when we accept that people are all individual, we have to acknowledge that some of them are assholes. Of course there is the nature versus nurture debate, but above and beyond all of that, some people are innately just not very nice. There, I've said it. I'm not calling all children assholes (and all the children of anyone who might read this are also exempt); I'm not even rolling out a percentage. I'm hedging my bets here. But every now and again I come across a child and think, 'Jeez, you really are a bit of an asshole.' I don't say it out loud, and I don't change my facial expression or my demeanour (I'm not completely crazy), but I think it.

The toddler at playgroup who ground my son's face into a Thomas the Tank Engine mat for no reason, and the one the week after who grabbed his rice cracker and stamped on it until it was dust. The wobbler in the playground who threw mud at my little boy because he coveted the swing he was on, and the five-year-old who kicked me in the shin at the bus stop. Assholes. The lot of them. And the worst thing is, you can't stand up to them or argue back, mainly because that would make you the bigger asshole (and might get you arrested), but also because it would be an exercise in futility. We all know from our own children that arguing with a toddler is like an Irish Eurovision entry after 1997 – pointless. And more often that not, attempting a polite discussion with a toddler's parent can prove as fruitless, because we all think our kids are the best. Any event involving a lot of parents and children in one place can turn into a bad prison drama when something goes wrong, because everyone is innocent.

I know that a child's world is essentially a more safeguarded version of the adult one they will one day wake up in (hey, we've all watched *The Secret Life of Four-Year-Olds*), that they have to learn from a young age that not everyone is going to be charm personified or have their back, and that some day, maybe in a job or a relationship, they will experience the adult equivalent of someone stamping on their rice cracker.

I know all of this, and as an adult, I have had my face metaphorically ground into a Thomas the Tank Engine mat more times than I care to remember (keep up, folks), but it doesn't stop me wanting to grab my son the second I see anyone not being lovely to him. Whilst he is still so little, I can do this without offending anyone or being accused of cotton-wool parenting, but the day will come when I can't scoop him up and take him away from anything that might upset him (because that would be weird when he's 23, right? RIGHT??), and I do understand that it's all just part of the life I need to prepare him for.

I'm also acutely aware that at least once in his life, someone might think he is the asshole. But let's not think about that now.

Of course, even the non-asshole kids have their moments, and I think we all know the unspoken rules about witnessing a toddler tantrum in public:

- Do not judge. It could happen to you.
- Do not scowl, roll your eyes or talk to the child about their mother in the third person. It could happen to you.
- It could happen to you.

And yet we have all been guilty of at least a surreptitious butt clench when we hear a stressed parent trying to console or control a toddler whose world is about to end because they can't have that giant bag of sweets/cuddly toy/bottle of toilet cleaner. Even though those of us who have kids try not to judge, we are quietly thankful that our children aren't that bad, thinking that we would approach the scenario differently, and oh-aren't-we-lucky-our-toddlers-don't-shriek-that-loudly, as we give the other mum the sympathetic 'we've all been there' look, but with added unintentional 'but your child might just be a little bit louder than mine' raised eyebrow.

Admit it. You've thought this.

Or at least you do until it happens to you. This first for me happened in a playgroup, and so was mortifyingly witnessed by lots of people I was hoping to see again. Tom was overtired, overwhelmed, and cried, thrashed and wailed like a tiny hungover banshee (which I imagine is far worse than the regular kind). Then he tried to grab someone else's sippy cup and I realised I had forgotten his. So not only was I now the owner of the screamer, but I was also the disorganised mother. Who the hell forgets to pack the sippy cup? (Response: someone who was up four times during the night, that's who).

When it happens to you, the reaction of others makes you accept that, yes, your toddler does caterwaul as loudly as other children, it's just that you happen to love this tiny wobbler throwing a wobbler, your inner ears have adjusted to their screams and, not unlike farts, other people's are always infinitely less bearable.

Feeling sorry for or pitying someone is not the same as having a true understanding of their plight. When you experience these situations first hand, that sympathy evolves into empathy. Empathy is the most important of human emotions and is what separates us from animals. OK, so that's completely untrue but I just liked the finality of it. Lots of things separate us from animals (but not always the same things, or even the good things - I refer you to teenage boys). Also animals on the whole are great and we could take many a leaf out of their furry books. So, let me rephrase that: empathy is what separates us from dickheads.

Empathy is the most complex kind of social intelligence, as it can be easy to fake in many circumstances, except in the case of parenting. The subtle nuances that exist between sympathy and empathy can be sniffed out a mile away by another parent. It might be in the tilt of a head, in the words you use, and it might be completely unintentional. But they will know if you genuinely understand or not.

Of course, in the grand scheme of things, it doesn't matter a jot. The parent and screaming toddler will leave, and the slightly patronising observers will go on their respective ways, and the whole debacle will be forgotten in minutes. But when I forgot that damn cup, I felt the difference between those who understood and those who just pretended to. And I will never, ever forget the fucking sippy cup again.

MILES TO GO BEFORE WE SLEEP

AS I WRITE this book, I am only in my third year of motherhood, and I know many of you reading it might have multiple children or be so far from the early stages of parenting that it's but a distant memory. Others might think, 'Jeez, that silly moo has far harder stuff ahead. Why the hell is she writing a book now?' I know there are many years of milestones, hurdles, the good, the bad and the catchment areas for schools ahead, but I think the experience of becoming a parent for the first time is so enormously significant that it warrants as much discussion from as many angles as possible.

I feel so different now than I did when my son was born, and I see just how much my friends who have three or four kids take things in their stride (and these are people who would have had a meltdown trying to decide between a chicken or lamb kebab at 3 a.m. not so long ago), so I think it's important to remind them that they're doing a brilliant job – just in case no one else does.

A new mother said to me recently, 'Isn't having a baby so hard? I wish someone had told me *just* how hard it would be.' Yes, it's damn hard. But if every new mum walked around with a thousand-yard stare warning others of the fate that awaited them, we'd have no new people and would probably have to rely on cloning and those creepy silicone dolls. And although it's difficult, the oft-abused cliché is true: it really is one of the best things in the world. If it's a step you decide to take, you will not regret it. But we live in a different world to our mothers and grandmothers. Many of us don't have the same support or don't live in a community where we can knock on our neighbours' doors. We live in an era of increased loneliness, stress, negative equity, endless social media pressure and uncertainty. It's important that we keep talking, and that's all I intended this book to be: a light-hearted part of a vital conversation. When I became a mother for the first time, I didn't need someone to tell me on a loop how hard it would be; I needed some fears allayed, some questions answered, some distraction and adult conversation, some tea and biscuits (or wine and crisps, depending on the time of day), and for someone to smile, nod, understand what I was talking about and tell me I wasn't making a complete mess of things.

We all have miles to go before we sleep, and having other women on our side along the way makes the journey so much better.

A LETTER TO TOM

—

DEAR TOM LAURENCE,

I'm never sure if these 'letters to the future' are a good idea, but sod it. If I change my mind, I'll just tear this bit out of any of the copies of this book you're likely to see. Who am I kidding - you will never read this book, but you may rip a page out one day to write a phone number on, so I'll keep that in mind.

Before I had you, I wasn't sure that being a mother was for me. There was so much else to do and I'd never be as good a mum as your Granny was anyway, so I thought maybe I'd be better off leaving it to others. I'm so glad I didn't. I hope I turn out to be as good a mum as you deserve, but it's impossible to put into words how glad

I am that you came into my life. We spent so much time together, just you and me, when you were tiny, and you were the best company I had ever kept. We had so many adventures that you won't remember (but I'll no doubt bore you with one day with the benefit of nostalgia whilst you roll your eyes and think, 'oh no, not the woman-on-the-plane story again'). You are amazing, and if anyone ever tells you otherwise, just give me their address and then clear the area.

I don't know what advice to give you as I don't know what you'll need or who you'll become, and I know I took very little of my parents' advice on board until I was about 30, so maybe I should have just stapled a €50 note to this page …

Or maybe I'll give it a go.

- Choice is a good thing, but not necessarily too much. It's easy to know what you don't want to do, but far more difficult to decide what you actually want to do.
- Ignore best-before dates – just use your nose.
- Never stay around people who make you feel bad about yourself, even if you are desperate for them to like, or love, you.
- Common sense trumps most other faculties.

- Look after your skin, even if you have to do it on the sly so no one will call you names – you'll have the last laugh.
- There's no such thing as 'the one that got away'; there are scores of potential 'ones' out there for you.
- Don't trust people who hate animals.
- Slow and steady doesn't always win the race; sometimes you need to make yourself heard.
- Never take credit for other people's work and don't let anyone take it for yours.
- Family is important, but so are friends – blood may be thicker than water, but sometimes I accept you might just need water.

I worry so much about you growing up in an era of always-on Internet, cyber-bullying, social media and Photoshop. I hope I'll teach you enough of the good stuff so that you will understand what matters and what really, really doesn't. I hope I manage to find ways to show you the importance of kindness, consent and empathy, and I hope I can help you reach whatever your full potential is.

Please don't sue me in years to come for putting those videos of you on Facebook. My account was set to private and just be thankful I never did set up that YouTube channel of you looking disappointed on hundreds of coin-operated rides.

And remember, wherever you are and whatever age you are, you can always, always come home. Just call first; I might be in Las Vegas. Or at the post office (hopefully just to get the money out for Vegas).

I love you.

Mum X

Acknowledgements

Thank you to my family for loving little Tom Laurence like I couldn't have imagined. To my siblings, Marc and Anna, and to my remarkable parents, Helen and Tom, for ... well, pretty much everything over the last four decades, but in more recent times, for minding the little man whilst this book was cobbled together.

To my Baby Daddy, Johnny, for the good genes. Isn't he just lovely? ;) And to my stepson, Michael, for all the Tom memes.

Thank you to all the supporters and everyone involved in The M Word, but especially Gary Finn, Seth Harkness, and the many brilliant women who share such personal stories with charm, flair and humour.

To Fearne Cotton for the lovely endorsement! You always take the time to be kind, gracious and champion other women when you have so many plates spinning yourself. Thank you.

Thank you to Deirdre Nolan, Catherine Gough, Teresa Daly and all at Gill Books for taking a chance with this. If it fails miserably, let's recycle the unsold books into overpriced Eco-Play Tree Houses before you pull an Alan Partridge and pulp them.